Certificate BA3

FUNDAMENTALS OF FINANCIAL ACCOUNTING

For assessments from 2017

Exam Practice Kit

In this edition

- Banks of objective test questions across the whole syllabus
- Answers with detailed feedback
- Advice on exam technique

First edition 2016
Second edition 2017

ISBN 9781 5097 1168 0
Previous ISBN 9781 5097 0641 9
eISBN 9781 5097 1180 2

British Library Cataloguing-in-Publication Data
A catalogue record for this book is available from the British Library

Published by

BPP Learning Media Ltd
BPP House, Aldine Place
142-144 Uxbridge Road
London W12 8AA

www.bpp.com/learningmedia

Printed in the United Kingdom

Your learning materials, published by BPP Learning Media Ltd, are printed on paper obtained from traceable sustainable sources.

Contents

Question and Answer index

Using your BPP Exam Practice Kit

One of the key criteria for achieving exam success is question practice. There is generally a direct correlation between candidates who study all topics and practise exam questions and those who are successful in their exams. This Kit gives you ample opportunity for such practice throughout your preparations for your OT exam.

All questions in your exam are compulsory and all the component learning outcomes will be examined so you must **study the whole syllabus**. Selective studying will limit the number of questions you can answer and hence reduce your chances of passing.

Practising as many exam-style questions as possible will be the key to passing this exam. You must do questions under **timed conditions** as part of your preparations.

Breadth of question coverage

Exam questions will test your knowledge of all areas of the syllabus. Therefore, it is important to revise all topics studied in the Course Book and Exam Practice Kit.

The weightings in the table below indicate the approximate proportion of study time you should spend on each topic, and is related to the number of questions per syllabus area in the exam.

BA3: Fundamentals of Financial Accounting	
Syllabus topics	**Weighting**
A Accounting Principles, Concepts and Regulations	10%
B Recording Accounting Transactions	50%
C Preparation of Accounts for Single Entities	30%
D Analysis of Financial Statements	10%

The Exam

The exam is a computer based assessment, which is available on demand at assessment centres all year round.

The exams at Certificate Level can be taken in any order, but candidates must pass or be exempt from them all before they can move on to the Operational Level.

Each exam lasts for two hours and will contain 60 questions.

The exam will be made up of different types of questions, as shown below:

Question Type	Explanation
Multiple choice	Standard multiple choice items provide four options. One option is correct and the other three are incorrect. Incorrect options will be plausible, so you should expect to have to use detailed, syllabus-specific knowledge to identify the correct answer rather than relying on common sense.
Multiple response	A multiple response item is the same as a multiple choice question, except more than one response is required. You will be told how many options you need to select.
Number entry	Number entry (or 'fill in the blank') questions require you to type a short numerical response. You should carefully follow the instructions in the question in terms of how to type your answer – eg the correct number of decimal places
Drag and drop	Drag and drop questions require you to drag a "token" onto a pre-defined area. These tokens can be images or text. This type of question is effective at testing the order of events, labelling a diagram or linking events to outcomes.
Hot spot	These questions require you to identify an area or location on an image by clicking on it. This is commonly used to identify a specific point on a graph or diagram.
Item set	2–4 questions all relating to the same short scenario. Each question will be 'standalone', such that your ability to answer subsequent questions in the set does not rely on getting the first one correct.

BPP
LEARNING MEDIA

Passing the Exam

- Read, and **re-read the question** to ensure you fully understand what is being asked.

- When starting to read a question, especially one with a lengthy scenario, **read the requirement first**. You will then find yourself considering the requirement as you read the data in the scenario, helping you to focus on exactly what you have to do.

- **Do not spend too much time on one question** – remember you should spend 2 minutes, on average, per question.

- If you cannot decide between two answers – look carefully and decide whether for one of the options you are making an unnecessary assumption – **do not be afraid of trusting your gut instinct.**

- **Do not keep changing your mind** – research has shown that the 1st answer that appeals to you is often the correct one.

- Remember that marks are awarded for correct answers, and marks will not be deducted for incorrect answers. Therefore **answer every single question**, even ones you are unsure of.

- Always submit an answer for a given question even if you do not know the answer – **never leave any answers blank.**

- **Pace yourself** – you will need to work through the exam at the right speed. Too fast and your accuracy may suffer, too slow and you may run out of time. Use this Kit to practise your time keeping and approach to answering each question.

- If you are unsure about anything, remember to **ask the test administrator** before the test begins.

- Remember to **keep moving on!** You may be presented with a question which you simply cannot answer due to difficulty or if the wording is too vague. If you find yourself spending five minutes determining the answer for a question then your time management skills are poor and you are wasting valuable time.

- If you finish the exam with time to spare, use the rest of the time to **review your answers** and to make sure that you answered every question.

Questions

1 The nature and objective of accounting

1   Which THREE of the following users of financial statements are likely to be interested in the final accounts of a small private company?

☐   Stock market analysts
☐   Company employees
☐   The company's bank
☐   Institutional shareholders
☐   Suppliers

2   According to IAS 1 *Presentation of financial statements* which TWO of the following are objectives of financial statements?

☐   To show the results of management's stewardship of the resources entrusted to it

☐   To provide a basis for valuing the entity

☐   To provide information about the financial position, financial performance and cash flows of an entity that is useful to a wide range of users in making economic decisions

☐   To facilitate comparison of financial performance between entities operating in different industries

☐   To assist management and those charged with governance in making timely economic decisions about deployment of the entity's resources

3   What does GAAP stand for?

A   Generally Agreed Accounting Policies
B   Generally Accepted Accounting Policies
C   Generally Agreed Accounting Practice
D   Generally Accepted Accounting Principles

4   Which TWO of the following information needs apply to the government and its agencies in relation to the business of a sole trader?

The government and its agencies need information to:

☐   Establish levels of tax revenue
☐   Assess whether the business will continue in existence
☐   Produce national statistics
☐   Assess the owner's stewardship
☐   Take decisions about their investment

5   In the UK which of the following are responsible for the preparation of company annual financial statements?

   A   The shareholders
   B   The board of directors
   C   The auditors
   D   The members

6   It has been suggested that there are seven separate user groups of published accounting statements. These include owner/investors, loan payables, analysts/advisors, business contacts (for example, customers and suppliers) and the public. Which two are missing?

   1   _____
   2   _____

7   How has the increasing complexity of modern business contributed to the development of accounting?

   A   Lenders need more information
   B   Government needs more information
   C   Too many transactions, so managers need a means of summarising them
   D   Too many transactions, so investors need a means of summarising them

8   Fill in the blanks.

   The main distinction between financial accounting and management accounting is that financial accounting provides _____ information to people _____ the organisation, whereas management accounting provides _____ information to _____ on which they can base _____.

9   Capital is?

   A   The amount borrowed to set up a business
   B   The amount owed by a business to its proprietor(s)
   C   The value of the assets in a business
   D   The total amount invested in a business by all the providers of capital

10 Which groups of people are most likely to be interested in the financial statements of a sole trader?

   1   Shareholders of the company
   2   The business bank manager
   3   The tax authorities
   4   Financial analysts

   A   1 and 2 only
   B   2 and 3 only
   C   2, 3 and 4 only
   D   1, 2 and 3 only

11   Which of the following statements is/are true?

1   The shareholder needs a statement of financial prospects, ie an indication of future progress. However, the supplier of goods on credit needs a statement of financial position, ie an indication of the current state of affairs.

2   The objective of financial statements is to provide information about the financial position, performance and changes in financial position of an entity that is useful to a wide range of users in making economic decisions.

A   1 only
B   2 only
C   Both 1 and 2
D   Neither 1 or 2

12   The purpose of the financial statement that lists an entity's total assets and total capital/liabilities is to show:

A   The financial performance of the entity over a period of time
B   The amount the entity could be sold for in the event of a liquidation
C   The amount the entity could be sold for as a going concern
D   The financial position of the entity at a particular moment in time

The following data relates to questions 13 to 15.

You are a trainee accountant at HTX Co, a start up company. Your boss, the managing director, has left you with some tasks to perform.

Firstly, he wants to hire both a management accountant and a financial accountant, and has asked you to prepare a job description for each role, based on his handwritten notes. However, he forgot to specify which of the following duties are for which role:

☐ Prepares accounts for internal use
☐ Prepares accounts for external use
☐ Prepares budgets
☐ Compares actual performance with budget
☐ Costs products
☐ Prepares accounts under IFRS
☐ Prepares the statement of financial position and statement of profit of loss
☐ Prepares historic accounts

He has also given you the following details of transactions for the month of April 20X1.

Sales

Invoice/transaction date	Inv No.	$
01.04.16	001	2,000
04.04.16	002	3,000
01.05.16	003	1,500

Purchases

Invoice/transaction date	Inv No.	$
05.04.16	X123	950
10.04.16	000999	3,500

13   Select which of the duties listed above are typically part of the role of a management accountant.

☐   Prepares accounts for internal use

☐   Prepares accounts for external use

☐   Prepares budgets

☐   Compares actual performance with budget

☐   Costs products

☐   Prepares accounts under IFRS

☐   Prepares the statement of financial position and statement of profit of loss

☐   Prepares historic accounts

14   Select which of the duties listed above are typically part of the role of a financial accountant.

☐   Prepares accounts for internal use

☐   Prepares accounts for external use

☐   Prepares budgets

☐   Compares actual performance with budget

☐   Costs products

☐   Prepares accounts under IFRS

☐   Prepares the statement of financial position and statement of profit of loss

☐   Prepares historic accounts

15   What was the profit for HTX Co for April under the accruals basis of accounting?

$ ☐

2 An introduction to final accounts

1   A sole trader borrows $10,000 from a bank.

Which elements of the accounting equation will change due to this transaction?

A   Assets and liabilities

B   Assets and capital

C   Capital and liabilities

D   Assets only

2   A sole trader sells goods for cash for $500 which had cost $300.

    Which elements of the accounting equation will change due to this transaction?

    A   Assets and liabilities
    B   Assets and capital
    C   Capital and liabilities
    D   Assets only

3   A sole trader increases the number of company motor vehicles by adding his own car to its fleet.

    Which elements of the accounting equation will change due to this transaction?

    A   Assets only
    B   Capital only
    C   Assets and capital
    D   Assets and liabilities

4   The profit made by a business in 20X7 was $35,400. The proprietor injected new capital of $10,200 during
    the year and withdrew a monthly salary of $500.

    If net assets at the end of 20X7 were $95,100, what was the proprietor's capital at the beginning of the year?

    A $50,000
    B $55,500
    C $63,900
    D $134,700

5   Which one of the following can the accounting equation be rewritten as?

    A   Assets + profit – drawings – liabilities = closing capital
    B   Assets – liabilities – drawings = opening capital + profit
    C   Assets – liabilities – opening capital + drawings = profit
    D   Assets – profit – drawings = closing capital – liabilities

6   A business had net assets at 1 January and 31 December 20X9 of $75,600 and $73,800 respectively. During
    the year, the proprietor introduced additional capital of $17,700 and withdrew cash and goods to the value of
    $16,300.

    What was the profit or loss made by the business in 20X9?

    A $3,200 loss
    B $3,200 profit
    C $400 loss
    D $400 profit

7   The accounting equation can be written as:

    A   Assets + profits – drawings – liabilities = closing capital
    B   Assets – liabilities – drawings = opening capital + profit
    C   Assets – liabilities – opening capital + drawings = profit
    D   Opening capital + profit – drawings – liabilities = assets

8   The capital of a sole trader would change as a result of:

A   A credit customer paying by cheque
B   Raw materials being purchased on credit
C   Non-current assets being purchased on credit
D   Personal petrol being paid for out of company petty cash

9   Which one of the following can the accounting equation can be rewritten as?

A   Assets + profit − drawings − liabilities = closing capital
B   Assets − liabilities − drawings = opening capital + profit
C   Assets − liabilities − opening capital + drawings = profit
D   Assets − profit − drawings = closing capital − liabilities

10   The profit earned by a business in 20X7 was $72,500. The proprietor injected new capital of $8,000 during the year and withdrew goods for his private use which had cost $2,200.

If net assets at the beginning of 20X7 were $101,700, what were the closing net assets?

A $35,000
B $39,400
C $168,400
D $180,000

11   A sole trader is $5,000 overdrawn at her bank and receives $1,000 from a credit customer in respect of its account.

Which elements of the accounting equation will change due to this transaction?

A   Assets and liabilities only
B   Liabilities only
C   Assets only
D   Assets, liabilities and capital

12   A sole trader purchases goods on credit.

Which elements of the accounting equation will change due to this transaction?

A   Assets and liabilities
B   Assets and capital
C   Capital and liabilities
D   Assets only

The following data relates to questions 13 to 15.

You are a trainee accountant at Mongoose Co. You are going through the purchase invoices for the month of April 20X1 to determine if any purchases need to be classified as capital expenditure.

You have identified the items that you think might be capital expenditure:

(i)   Purchase of a 3D printer
(ii)   Repairing a broken window
(iii)   Extension of the office building
(iv)   Purchase of computer hardware
(v)   Purchase of ink for printers
        All of the above items were purchased on credit and have not been paid for at the end of the month.

13   Which of the items should be classified as capital expenditure?

    A   (i), (ii) and (iii)
    B   (ii) and (iv)
    C   (i) (iii) and (iv)
    D   (i) (iv) and (v)

14   In which of the following categories of the statement of financial position should the capital expenditure items above be included?

    A   Current assets
    B   Non-current assets
    C   Capital
    D   Retained earnings

15   What other ledger account will be affected by the capital expenditure purchases in April 20X1?

    A   Trade receivables
    B   Trade payables
    C   Bank
    D   Revenue

3 Sources, records and the books of prime entry

1   Which of the following best explains the imprest system of petty cash?

    A   Each month an equal amount of cash is transferred into petty cash
    B   The exact amount of petty cash expenditure is reimbursed at intervals to maintain a fixed float
    C   Petty cash must be kept under lock and key
    D   The petty cash total must never fall below the imprest amount

2   Which of the following is a book of original entry?

    A   Nominal ledger
    B   Journal
    C   Receivables ledger
    D   Asset register

3   When a purchase invoice is received from a supplier, which TWO of the following documents would the invoice be checked to?

☐ Sales order
☐ Purchase order
☐ Remittance advice
☐ Goods received note
☐ Credit note

4   In which book of original entry would discounts allowed be recorded?

A   Sales day book
B   Purchases day book
C   Cash book
D   Journal

5   In which book of original entry is VAT on credit sales recorded?

A   Sales day book
B   Purchases day book
C   Cash book
D   Journal

6   Which of the following documents should accompany a return of goods to a supplier?

A   Debit note
B   Remittance advice
C   Purchase invoice
D   Credit note

7   Which of the following are books of prime entry?

1   Sales day book
2   Cash book
3   Journal
4   Purchase ledger

A   1 and 2 only
B   1, 2 and 3 only
C   1 only
D   All of them

8   In which book of prime entry will a business record credit notes in respect of goods which have been sent back to suppliers?

A   The cash book
B   The purchase returns day book
C   The purchase day book
D   The sales returns day book

9   Which of the following would be recorded in the sales day book?

   A   Discounts allowed
   B   Sales invoices
   C   Credit notes received
   D   Trade discounts

10   Which prime entry record is used to record credit notes for returns outwards?

   A   Sales returns day book
   B   The journal
   C   The cash book
   D   The purchase returns day book

11   Which one of the following source documents is summarised and posted to the general ledger?

   A   Sales returns day book
   B   Purchases day book
   C   Cash receipts book
   D   The purchase returns day book

12   Which prime entry record is used to record direct debits to pay utility bills?

   A   Sales returns day book
   B   The journal
   C   The cash payments book
   D   The purchase returns day book

The following data relates to questions 13 to 15.

You are an accounts assistant for Klemspeck Solutions, a company that sells computer equipment.

The following transactions took place on 23 January 20X1:

		$
(i)	Cash sale of goods to Customers A Davis	200
(ii)	Credit sale of goods to Customer H Tyre	150
(iii)	Return of goods from Customer B Rudd	30
(iv)	Payment to supplier Z Computers	900
(v)	Purchase invoice from supplier Z Computers	150
(vi)	Purchase of stationary with petty cash	10

13   Which of the above transactions would be recorded in the purchases day book?

   A   (vi)
   B   (iv) and (v)
   C   (v)
   D   (iv) and (vi)

14   Which of the above transactions would be recorded in the sales day book?

    A   (i)
    B   (ii)
    C   (iii)
    D   (ii) and (iii)

15   Which of the above transactions would be recorded in the cash book?

    A   (i) and (iv)
    B   (iv) and (vi)
    C   (i), (iv) and (vi)
    D   (iii), (iv) and (vi)

4 Ledger accounting and double entry

1   A credit balance in a ledger account would normally be shown where the account is:

    (i)   An asset account
    (ii)   A liability account
    (iii)   A capital account
    (iv)   An income account
    (v)   An expense account

    A   (ii) and (iv) only
    B   (i), (iii) and (v) only
    C   (ii), (iii) and (iv) only
    D   (ii), (iii) and (v) only

2   A debit entry to the sales account could represent:

    A   The correction of an error or goods returned
    B   Irrecoverable debts written off
    C   Credit sales
    D   Cash sales

3   This question examines your use of debits and credits in relation to accounts in the nominal ledger.

    Ignoring the other side of an entry, which THREE of the following are true?

    ☐   Incurring an expense results in a debit to the expense account
    ☐   Decrease in a liability results in a debit to the liability account
    ☐   Increase in an asset results in a credit to the asset account
    ☐   Decrease in an asset results in a debit to the asset account
    ☐   Increase in a liability results in a credit to the liability account

4   An accountant has inserted all the relevant figures into the trade payables account, but has not yet balanced off the account.

TRADE PAYABLES ACCOUNT

	$		$
Cash at bank	100,750	Balance b/d	250,225
		Purchases	325,010

Assuming there are no other entries to be made, other than to balance off the account, what is the closing balance on the trade payables account?

A $474,485 DR
B $575,235 DR
C $474,485 CR
D $575,235 CR

5   How is the total of the purchases day book posted to the nominal ledger?

A   Debit purchases, Credit Cash and bank
B   Debit payables control, Credit purchases
C   Debit Cash and bank, Credit purchases
D   Debit purchases, Credit payables control

6   The nominal ledger is:

A   A record of amounts owed to/from individual suppliers and customers
B   An initial record of internally generated transactions
C   A list of all assets and liabilities at a point in time
D   A collection of accounts recording all the transactions of the business

7   A credit would not result in which of the following?

A   Increase in a liability
B   Increase in an asset
C   Increase in capital
D   Increase in income

8   In double entry bookkeeping, which of the following statements is true?

A   Credit entries decrease expenses and increase assets
B   Credit entries decrease liabilities and increase income
C   Debit entries decrease income and increase assets
D   Debit entries decrease expenses and increase assets

9   Jones Co. has the following transactions:

1   Payment of $400 to J Bloggs for a cash purchase
2   Payment of $250 to J Doe in respect of an invoice for goods purchased last month

What are the correct ledger entries to record these transactions?

A   DR Cash and bank $650
          CR Purchases $650

B   DR Purchases $650
          CR Cash and bank $650

C   DR Purchases $400
      DR Trade payables $250
          CR Cash and bank $650

D   DR Cash and bank $650
          CR Trade payables $250
          CR Purchases $400

---

10   Tin Co purchases $250 worth of metal from Steel Co. Tin Co agrees to pay Steel Co. in 60 days' time.

What is the double entry to record the purchase in Steel Co's books?

A   Debit sales $250, credit receivables $250
B   Debit purchases $250, credit payables $250
C   Debit receivables $250, credit sales $250
D   Debit payables $250, credit purchases $250

---

11   T Tallon had the following transactions:

(i)   Sale of goods on credit for $150 to F Rogit
(ii)   Return of goods from B Blendigg originally sold for $300 in cash to B Blendigg

What are the correct ledger entries to record these transactions?

A   DR Trade receivables $150
      DR Sales Returns $300
          CR Revenue $150
          CR Cash and bank $300

B   DR Revenue $150
      DR Cash and bank $300
          CR Trade receivables $150
          CR Sales Returns $300

C   DR Trade receivables $450
          CR Revenue $150
          CR Sales Returns $300

D   DR Sales Returns $300
      DR Revenue $150
          CR Cash and bank $450

12   The suppliers' personal accounts will appear in which of the following business records?

    A   The nominal ledger
    B   The sales ledger
    C   The purchase day book
    D   The purchase ledger

The following data relates to questions 13 to 15

You are a trainee accountant at KLS Ltd and have discovered that the following items were omitted from the books of prime entry:

- Cash sale of $50
- Purchase of office chairs for $1,000
- Credit sales of $450

13   Prepare a journal entry to account for the cash sale omitted from the books of prime entry.

    DEBIT   _____ $50
    CREDIT _____ $50

14   Prepare a journal entry to account for the purchase of office chairs omitted from the books of prime entry.

    DEBIT   _____ $1,000
    CREDIT _____ $1,000

15   Prepare a journal entry to account for the credit sale omitted from the books of prime entry.

    The double entry to record a credit sale is:

    DEBIT   _____ $450
    CREDIT _____ $450

5 From trial balance to final accounts

1   Which of the following statements is incorrect?

    A   The closing inventory balance is included in the trial balance
    B   If the trial balance does not balance, an error must have been made
    C   The opening inventory balance is included in the trial balance
    D   Proprietors' drawings are shown on the trial balance

2   When preparing a trial balance, the clerk omits the balance of $2,000 on the receivables account. This error means that the total of debit balances will exceed the total of credit balances by $2,000.

    A   True
    B   False

3   A business has the following extract from its trial balance:

	$
Trade receivables	5,000
Bank overdraft	2,000
Trade payables	7,000
Inventory	4,500

What is the figure for current assets?

A $9,500
B $7,000
C $11,500
D $9,000

4   Where a transaction is entered into the correct ledger accounts, but the wrong amount is used, what is the error known as?

A   An error of omission
B   An error of original entry
C   An error of commission
D   An error of principle

5   Which of the following errors would cause a trial balance not to balance?

1   An error in the addition in the cash book

2   Failure to record a transaction at all

3   Cost of a motor vehicle debited to motor expenses account. The cash entry was correctly made

4   Goods taken by the proprietor of a business recorded by debiting purchases and crediting drawings account

A   1 only
B   1 and 2 only
C   3 and 4 only
D   All four items

6   An organisation restores its petty cash balance to $250 at the end of each month. During October, the total expenditure column in the petty cash book was calculated as being $210, and the imprest was restored by this amount. The analysis columns posted to the nominal ledger totalled only $200.

Which one of the following would this error cause?

A   The trial balance being $10 higher on the debit side
B   The trial balance being $10 higher on the credit side
C   No imbalance in the trial balance
D   The petty cash balance being $10 lower than it should be

7   A purchase return of $48 has been wrongly posted to the debit of the sales returns account, but has been correctly entered in the supplier's account.

   Which of the following statements about the trial balance would be correct?

   A   The credit side to be $48 more than the debit side
   B   The debit side to be $48 more than the credit side
   C   The credit side to be $96 more than the debit side
   D   The debit side to be $96 more than the credit side

8   Two types of common errors in bookkeeping are errors of **principle** and errors of **transposition**.

   Which of the following correctly states whether or not these errors will be revealed by extracting a trial balance?

	Errors of principle	Errors of transposition
A	Will be revealed	Will not be revealed
B	Will be revealed	Will be revealed
C	Will not be revealed	Will not be revealed
D	Will not be revealed	Will be revealed

9   Bert has extracted the following list of balances from his general ledger at 31 October 20X5:

	$
Revenue	258,542
Opening inventory	9,649
Purchases	124,958
Expenses	34,835
Non-current assets (carrying amount)	63,960
Trade receivables	31,746
Trade payables	13,864
Cash at bank	1,783
Capital	12,525

   What is the total of the debit balances in Bert's trial balance at 31 October 20X5?

   A $266,931
   B $275,282
   C $283,148
   D $284,931

10   What is an error of commission?

   A   An error where a transaction has not been recorded

   B   An error where one side of a transaction has been recorded in the wrong account, and that account is of a different class to the correct account

   C   An error where one side of a transaction has been recorded in the wrong account, and that account is of the same class as the correct account

   D   An error where the numbers in the posting have been transposed

11 Which THREE of the following sets of items all appear on the same side of the trial balance?

1   Sales, interest received and accruals
2   Trade receivables, drawings and discount received
3   Non-current assets, cost of sales and carriage outwards
4   Capital, trade payables and other operating expenses
5   Sundry expenses, prepayments and purchases

A   1, 4 and 5
B   1, 3 and 5
C   1, 2 and 3
D   3, 4 and 5

---

12 Which of the following errors would result in a trial balance failing to agree?

A   Failing to record an invoice from a supplier in the accounting system

B   Recording a non-current asset purchase as an item of revenue expenditure

C   Recording an expense payment as:
     DR Cash and bank CR expense a/c

D   Recording an expense payment as:
     DR expense a/c DR Cash and bank

The following information is relevant for Questions 13 to 15.

You work for JKL Ltd, a plumbing business. On 30.3.X6, the business had the following trial balance:

	$	$
Cash and bank	3,255	
Capital		15,500
Rent	2,225	
Trade payables		14,450
Purchases	13,150	
Revenue		14,600
Other payables		1,620
Trade receivables	12,000	
Other expenses	13,520	
Vehicles	2,020	
Total	46,170	46,170

The following transactions took place on 31.3.X7:

(i)   Purchase of materials for $100 by cheque
(ii)   Sale of goods to Customer Y for $500 credit

13   What is the double entry to record transaction (i)?

    A   DEBIT   Other expenses $100
            CREDIT   Bank $100

    B   DEBIT   Other expenses $100
            CREDIT   Trade payables $100

    C   DEBIT   Purchases $100
            CREDIT   Trade payables $100

    D   DEBIT   Purchases $100
            CREDIT   Bank $100

14   What is the double entry to record transaction (ii)?

    A   DEBIT   Bank $500
            CREDIT   Revenue $500

    B   DEBIT   Revenue $500
            CREDIT   Bank $500

    C   DEBIT   Trade receivables $500
            CREDIT   Revenue $500

    D   DEBIT   Revenue $500
            CREDIT   Trade receivables $500

15   Prepare the trial balance at 31.3.X7.

	$	$
Cash and bank		
Capital		
Rent		
Trade payables		
Purchases		
Revenue		
Other payables		
Trade receivables		
Other expenses		
Vehicles		
Total		

6 Tangible non-current assets

1   Is the following statement true or false?

'The balance per the non-current asset register always agrees with the balances per the non-current asset nominal ledgers.'

A   True
B   False

2   B purchased a machine for $120,000 on 1 October 20X1. The estimated useful life of the machine is four years, with a residual value of $4,000. B uses the straight-line method for depreciation and charges depreciation on a monthly basis.

What is the charge for depreciation for the year ended 31 December 20X1?

A $7,250
B $7,500
C $29,000
D $30,000

3   The year end for ABC is July 20X2 and in that month, a company car was stolen. The carrying value of the company car was $8,000, but the company expects the insurance company to pay only $6,000. The correct journal entry to record this information was entered in the books in July 20X2. In August 20X2, the insurance company sent a cheque for $6,500.

The journal entry to record this is:

		Dr $	Cr $
A	Bank	6,500	
	Sundry receivable		6,500
B	Bank	6,500	
	Sundry receivable		6,000
	Disposal of non-current assets account		500
C	Bank	500	
	Disposal of non-current assets account		500
D	Bank	500	
	Sundry receivable		500

4   S purchased equipment for $80,000 on 1 July 20X2. The company's accounting year end is 31 December. It is S's policy to charge a full year's depreciation in the year of purchase. S depreciates its equipment on the reducing balance basis at 25% per annum.

The carrying value of the equipment at 31 December 20X5 should be:

A   Nil
B $25,312
C $29,531
D $33,750

5   E bought computer equipment on 1 January 20X0 for $24,000 and estimated that it would have a useful life of five years and a residual value of $2,000. E uses the straight line method of depreciation. On 31 December 20X1, it now considers that the remaining life is only two years and that the residual value will be nil.

What should be the annual depreciation charge for the years ended 31 December 20X2 and 20X3?

A $2,800
B $5,500
C $6,600
D $7,600

6   Depreciation is best described as:

A   A means of spreading the payment for non-current assets over a period of years
B   A decline in the market value of the assets
C   A means of spreading the net cost of non-current assets over their estimated useful life
D   A means of estimating the amount of money needed to replace the assets

7   A business has made a profit of $8,000 but its bank balance has fallen by $5,000. This could be due to:

A   Depreciation of $3,000 and an increase in inventory of $10,000
B   Depreciation of $6,000 and the repayment of a loan of $7,000
C   Depreciation of $12,000 and the purchase of new non-current assets for $25,000
D   The disposal of a non-current asset for $13,000 less than its carrying value

8   A machine cost $9,000. It has an expected useful life of six years, and an expected residual value of $1,000. It is to be depreciated at 30% per annum on the reducing balance basis. A full year's depreciation is charged in the year of purchase, with none in the year of sale. During year 4, it is sold for $3,000.

The profit or loss on disposal is _____.

9   The accounting concept which dictates that non-current assets should be valued at cost, less accumulated depreciation, rather than their enforced saleable value, is the _____ concept.

10   A non-current asset was disposed of for $2,200 during the last accounting year. It had been purchased exactly three years earlier for $5,000, with an expected residual value of $500, and had been depreciated on the reducing balance basis, at 20% per annum.

The profit or loss on disposal was _____.

11   By charging depreciation in the accounts, a business aims to ensure that the cost of non-current assets is spread _____ which benefit from their use.

12   A business has a year end of 31 December.

A machine was purchased on 1 May 20X5 for $64,000. It was expected to last for 5 years and to have a residual value of $2,000. Depreciation was charged at 50% per annum on the reducing balance method, with a full year's charge in the year of purchase. No depreciation is charged in the year of disposal.

The machine was sold on 3 April 20X9 for $5,500. The profit or loss on the sale is

_____.

The following data relates to questions 13 to 15

You are a trainee accountant working for TYL Ltd. The company has an accounting year end of 31 December.

On 1 January 20X1, the business purchased a laser printer costing $1,800. The printer has an estimated life of 4 years, after which it will have no residual value. The managing director is unsure how to account for depreciation on the printer.

13   The managing director has asked you what the purpose of charging depreciation on non-current assets is. It is to:

    A   Put money aside to replace the assets when required
    B   Show the assets in the statement of financial position at their current market value
    C   Ensure that the profit is not understated
    D   Spread the net cost of the assets over their estimated useful life

14   Calculate the depreciation charge for the year ended 20X2 on the laser printer on the straight line basis:

    20X2 depreciation charge = _____

15   Calculate the depreciation charge for the year ended 20X2 on the laser printer on the reducing balance basis at 60% per annum:

    20X2 depreciation charge = _____

7 Intangible non-current assets

1   According to IAS 38 *Intangible assets,* which of the following statements about intangible assets are correct?

    1   If certain criteria are met, research expenditure must be recognised as an intangible asset.
    2   If certain criteria are met, development expenditure must be capitalised.
    3   Intangible assets must be amortised if they have a definite useful life.

    A   2 and 3 only
    B   1 and 3 only
    C   1 and 2 only
    D   All three statements are correct

2   According to IAS 38 *Intangible assets,* which of the following statements concerning the accounting treatment of research and development expenditure are true?

    1   If certain criteria are met, research expenditure may be recognised as an asset.

    2   Research expenditure, other than capital expenditure on research facilities, should be recognised as an expense as incurred.

    3   In deciding whether development expenditure qualifies to be recognised as an asset, it is necessary to consider whether there will be adequate finance available to complete the project.

    4   Development expenditure recognised as an asset must be amortised over a period not exceeding five years.

5   The financial statements should disclose the total amount of research and development expenditure recognised as an expense during the period.

    A   1, 4 and 5
    B   2, 4 and 5
    C   2, 3 and 4
    D   2, 3 and 5

---

3   According to IAS 38 *Intangible assets,* which of the following statements are correct?

    1   Research expenditure previously recognised as an expense should be recognised as an asset once development activities take place.

    2   Intangible assets are never amortised.

    3   Development expenditure must be capitalised if certain conditions are met.

    A   3 only
    B   1 and 2
    C   2 and 3
    D   All three statements are correct

---

4   Theta Co. purchased a patent on 1 December 20X3 for $25,000. Theta Co. expects to use the patent for the next ten years, after which it will have zero value. According to IAS 38 *Intangible assets,* what is the value of the patent in Theta Co's statement of financial position as at 30 November 20X5?

    A $25,000
    B $20,000
    C $5,000
    D $15,000

---

5   PF purchased a quota for carbon dioxide emissions for $15,000 on 1 May 20X6 and capitalised it as an intangible asset in its statement of financial position. PF estimates that the quota will have a useful life of 3 years. What is the journal entry required to record the amortisation of the quota in the accounts for the year ended 30 April 20X9?

    A   DR Expenses $15,000
            CR Accumulated amortisation $15,000

    B   DR Expenses $5,000
            CR Accumulated amortisation $5,000

    C   DR Intangible assets $5,000
            CR Accumulated amortisation $5,000

    D   DR Accumulated amortisation $15,000
            CR Intangible assets $15,000

---

6   Which ONE of the following is NOT an intangible non-current asset?

    A   Goodwill
    B   Trademark
    C   Investment
    D   Patent

7   According to IAS 38 *Intangible assets*, which of the following statements about research and development expenditure are correct?

1   Research expenditure, other than capital expenditure on research facilities, should be recognised as an expense as incurred.

2   In deciding whether development expenditure qualifies to be recognised as an asset, it is necessary to consider whether there will be adequate finance available to complete the project.

3   Development expenditure recognised as an asset must be amortised over a period not exceeding five years.

A   1, 2 and 3
B   1 and 2 only
C   1 and 3 only
D   2 and 3 only

---

8   According to IAS 38 *Intangible assets*, which of the following statements about research and development expenditure are correct?

1   If certain conditions are met, an entity may decide to capitalise development expenditure.

2   Research expenditure, other than capital expenditure on research facilities, must be written off as incurred.

3   Capitalised development expenditure must be amortised over a period not exceeding five years.

4   Capitalised development expenditure must be disclosed in the statement of financial position under intangible non-current assets.

A   1, 2 and 4 only
B   1 and 3 only
C   2 and 4 only
D   3 and 4 only

---

9   According to IAS 38 *Intangible assets*, which of the following statements concerning the accounting treatment of research and development expenditure are true?

1   Development costs recognised as an asset must be amortised over a period not exceeding five years.

2   Research expenditure, other than capital expenditure on research facilities, should be recognised as an expense as incurred.

3   In deciding whether development expenditure qualifies to be recognised as an asset, it is necessary to consider whether there will be adequate finance available to complete the project.

4   Development projects must be reviewed at each reporting date, and expenditure on any project no longer qualifying for capitalisation must be amortised through the statement of profit or loss and other comprehensive income over a period not exceeding five years.

A   1 and 4
B   2 and 4
C   2 and 3
D   1 and 3

---

10   According to IAS 38 *Intangible assets*, which of the following statements is/are correct?

1   Capitalised development expenditure must be amortised over a period not exceeding five years.

2   If all the conditions specified in IAS 38 are met, development expenditure may be capitalised if the directors decide to do so.

3   Capitalised development costs are shown in the statement of financial position under the heading of non-current assets.

4   Amortisation of capitalised development expenditure will appear as an item in a company's statement of changes in equity.

A   3 only
B   2 and 3
C   1 and 4
D   1 and 3

11   According to IAS 38 *Intangible assets*, which of the following are intangible non-current assets in the accounts of Iota Co.?

1   A patent for a new glue purchased for $20,000 by Iota Co
2   Development costs capitalised in accordance with IAS 38
3   A licence to broadcast a television series, purchased by Iota Co. for $150,000
4   A state-of-the-art factory purchased by Iota Co. for $1.5 million

A   1 and 3 only
B   1, 2 and 3 only
C   2 and 4 only
D   2, 3 and 4 only

12   Which of the following items (that all generate future economic benefits, and whose costs can be measured reliably), is an intangible non-current asset?

1   Computer hardware owned by a business
2   Machinery
3   A patent bought by a business
4   An extension to an office building owned by a business

A   All four items
B   1, 2 and 4 only
C   1 and 2 only
D   3 only

The following information is relevant for questions 13 to 15.

You have recently joined Koppa Co. as a trainee accountant. The managing director has given you the following records prepared by your predecessor.

The following balances existed in the accounting records of Koppa Co. at 31 December 20X7.

	$'000
Development costs capitalised, 1 January 20X7	180
Research and development expenditure for the year	162

In preparing the company's statement of profit or loss and other comprehensive income and statement of financial position at 31 December 20X7, the following further information is relevant.

(a)   The $180,000 total for development costs as at 1 January 20X7 relates to two projects:

	$'000
Project 836: completed project	82
(balance being amortised over the period expected to benefit from it.	
Amount to be amortised in 20X7: $20,000)	
Project 910: in progress	98
	180

(b)   The research and development expenditure for the year is made up of:

	$'000
Research expenditure	103
Development costs on Project 910 which continues to satisfy the	
requirements in IAS 38 for capitalisation	59
	162

13   The managing director has asked you what the purpose of amortisation is. It is:

A   To allocate the cost of an intangible non-current asset over its useful life

B   To ensure that funds are available for the eventual purchase of a replacement non-current asset

C   To reduce the cost of an intangible non-current asset in the statement of financial position to its estimated market value

D   To account for the risk associated with intangible assets

14   According to IAS 38 *Intangible assets*, what amount should be charged in the statement of profit or loss and other comprehensive income for research and development costs for the year ended 31 December 20X7?

A $123,000
B $182,000
C $162,000
D $103,000

15   According to IAS 38 *Intangible assets*, what amount should be disclosed as an intangible asset in the statement of financial position for the year ended 31 December 20X7?

A $219,000
B $180,000
C $160,000
D $59,000

8 Cost of goods sold and inventories

1   Opening inventory of raw materials was $58,000, closing inventory was $63,000, purchases were $256,000, purchase returns were $17,000. What was cost of sales?

    A $256,000
    B $234,000
    C $239,000
    D $244,000

2   FIFO, LIFO and average cost are inventory valuation methods. Which of the following statements is correct?

    A   When prices are rising, FIFO will produce the higher profit figure of all these methods.
    B   When prices are rising, LIFO will produce the higher profit figure of all these methods.
    C   LIFO is a permissible valuation method under IAS 2.
    D   Average cost is recomputed following every dispatch or issue of inventory.

3   A company which gives its sales personnel 5% of sales price as commission, has the following inventory at the year end:

	Quantity	Cost	Per unit Estimated sales price
Beads	2,000	$1.50	$1.53
Buttons	1,500	$1.25	$1.40
Bows	2,000	$1.60	$1.50

At what value should this inventory be recorded in the final accounts?

    A $7,756
    B $7,632
    C $7,875
    D $8,175

4   A company values its inventory using the first in, first out (FIFO) method. At 1 May 20X2, the company had 700 engines in inventory, valued at $190 each.

During the year ended 30 April 20X3, the following transactions took place:

20X2
1 July   Purchased 500 engines at $220 each
1 November   Sold 400 engines for $160,000

20X3
1 February   Purchased 300 engines at $230 each
15 April   Sold 250 engines for $125,000

What is the value of the company's closing inventory of engines at 30 April 20X3?

    A $188,500
    B $195,500
    C $166,000
    D $187,500

5   You are preparing the final accounts for a business. The cost of the items in closing inventory is $41,875. This includes some items which cost $1,960 and which were damaged in transit. You have estimated that it will cost $360 to repair the items, and they can then be sold for $1,200.

What is the correct inventory valuation for inclusion in the final accounts?

A $39,915
B $40,755
C $41,515
D $42,995

6   What is the correct journal to record closing inventory in the nominal ledger at the year end?

A   Debit purchases (SPL), credit closing inventory (SOFP)
B   Debit closing inventory (cost of sales, SPL), credit closing inventory (SOFP)
C   Debit closing inventory (SOFP), credit closing inventory (cost of sales, SPL)
D   Debit sales (SPL), credit closing inventory (SOFP)

7   Opening inventory was $30,000, closing inventory was $34,000, purchases were $296,000 and carriage inwards was $11,000. What was cost of sales?

A $311,000
B $303,000
C $360,000
D $371,000

8   A company has an annual inventory count, the factory did not cease production during the inventory count and some goods in work in progress (cost $5,500) were later counted again and included in finished goods inventory (cost $7,500). As a result profit was?

A   Overstated by $2,000
B   Overstated by $7,500
C   Overstated by $5,500
D   Overstated by $13,000

9   Closing inventories are deducted from purchases and opening inventories in the statement of profit or loss in order to determine the cost of sales. Of which accounting concept is this an example?

_____

10 IAS 2 recognises two main ways of calculating cost of inventories. What are they? Complete the blanks below.

1   _____
2   _____

11 Gross profit for 20X3 can be calculated from:

A   Purchases for 20X3, plus inventory at 31 December 20X3, less inventory at 1 January 20X3
B   Purchases for 20X3, less inventory at 31 December 20X3, plus inventory at 1 January 20X3
C   Cost of goods sold during 20X3, plus sales during 20X3
D   Net profit for 20X3, plus expenses for 20X3

12   Which of the following methods of valuing inventory are allowed under IAS 2 *Inventories*?

    (i)   LIFO
    (ii)   Average cost
    (iii)   FIFO

    A   (i), (ii), and (iii)
    B   (i), (ii)
    C   (ii), (iii)
    D   (i), (iii)

The following data relates to questions 13 to 15.

You are a bookkeeper for a business that has recently commenced trading. The material used in the business, item Z, is subject to regular price rises.

The information below relates to inventory item Z.

March 1   50 units held in opening inventory at a cost of $40 per unit
      17   50 units purchased at a cost of $50 per unit
      31   60 units sold at a selling price of $100 per unit

Your boss, the managing director, is unsure of how to value the inventory and is trying to decide whether to use first in, first out (FIFO), or the cumulative weighted average pricing method.

13   Which of the following statements is correct?

    A   Profit will be unaffected by the method of inventory valuation.
    B   FIFO will lead to a higher reported profit.
    C   Continuous weighted average will lead to a higher reported profit.
    D   The profit figure will be more accurate if FIFO is used.

14   Under the first in first out method (FIFO), what is the value of inventory held for item Z at the end of March 31?

    A $4,000
    B $1,800
    C $2,000
    D $2,500

15   Under the cumulative weighted average pricing method, what is the value of inventory held for item Z at the end of March 31?

    A $4,000
    B $1,800
    C $2,000
    D $2,500

9 Irrecoverable debts and allowances for receivables

1   At 1 July 20X2, the receivables allowance of Q was $18,000.

During the year ended 30 June 20X3, debts totalling $14,600 were written off. It was determined that the receivables allowance should be $16,000 as at 30 June 20X3.

What amount should appear in Q's statement of profit or loss for receivables expense for the year ended 30 June 20X3?

A $12,600
B $16,600
C $48,600
D $30,600

2   At 31 December 20X4, a company's trade receivables totalled $864,000 and the allowance for receivables was $48,000.

It was determined that debts totalling $13,000 were to be written off, and the allowance for receivables adjusted to 5% of the receivables.

What figures should appear in the statement of financial position for trade receivables (after deducting the allowance) and in the statement of profit or loss for receivables expense?

	Statement of profit or loss $	Statement of financial position $
A	8,200	807,800
B	7,550	808,450
C	18,450	808,450
D	55,550	808,450

3   A company has been notified that a customer has been declared bankrupt. The company had previously made an allowance for this debt. Which of the following is the correct double entry to account for this new information?

	Debit	Credit
A	Irrecoverable debts	Receivables
B	Receivables	Irrecoverable debts
C	Allowance for receivables	Receivables
D	Receivables	Allowance for receivables

4   An increase in an allowance for receivables of $8,000 has been treated as a reduction in the allowance in the financial statements. Which of the following explains the resulting effects?

A   Net profit is overstated by $16,000, receivables overstated by $8,000
B   Net profit understated by $16,000, receivables understated by $16,000
C   Net profit overstated by $16,000, receivables overstated by $16,000
D   Gross profit overstated by $16,000, receivables overstated by $16,000

5   At 1 January 20X1, there was an allowance for receivables of $3,000. During the year, $1,000 of debts were written off as irrecoverable, and $800 of debts previously written off were recovered. At 31 December 20X1, it was determined that the allowance for receivables should be adjusted to 5% of receivables, which are $20,000.

What is the total receivables expense for the year?

A $200 debit
B $1,800 debit
C $2,200 debit
D $1,800 credit

---

6   A decrease in the allowance for receivables would result in:

A   An increase in liabilities
B   A decrease in working capital
C   A decrease in net profit
D   An increase in net profit

---

7   At the beginning of the year, the allowance for receivables was $850. At the year end, the allowances required was $1,000. During the year, $500 of debts were written off.

What is the charge to statement of profit or loss for irrecoverable debts for receivables for the year?

A $1,500
B $1,000
C $650
D $550

---

8   At 31 December 20X2, a company's receivables totalled $400,000 and an allowance for receivables of $50,000 had been brought forward from the year ended 31 December 20X1.

It was decided to write off debts totalling $38,000 and to adjust the allowance for receivables to 10% of the receivables.

What charge for receivables expense should appear in the company's statement of profit or loss for the year ended 31 December 20X2?

A $74,200
B $51,800
C $28,000
D $24,200

---

9   At 1 July 20X3, a limited liability company had an allowance for receivables of $83,000.

During the year ended 30 June 20X4, debts totalling $146,000 were written off. At 30 June 20X4, it was decided that a receivables allowance of $218,000 was required.

What figure should appear in the company's statement of profit or loss for the year ended 30 June 20X4 for receivables expense?

A $155,000
B $364,000
C $281,000
D $11,000

10   A company has received cash for a debt that was previously written off.

Which of the following is the correct double entry to record the cash received?

	Debit	Credit
A	Irrecoverable debts expense	Accounts receivable
B	Cash and bank	Irrecoverable debts expense
C	Allowance for receivables	Accounts receivable
D	Cash and bank	Allowance for receivables

11   Top Co has total receivables outstanding of $280,000. The accountant has determined that 1% of these balances will not be collected, so wishes to make an allowance of $28,000. No previous allowance has been made for receivables.

Which of the following is the correct double entry to create this allowance?

	Debit	Credit
A	Irrecoverable debts	Allowance for receivables
B	Allowance for receivables	Receivables
C	Irrecoverable debts	Receivables
D	Receivables	Allowance for receivables

12   At 30 September 20X2, a company's allowance for receivables amounted to $38,000, which was equivalent to 5% of the receivables at that date.

At 30 September 20X3, receivables totalled $868,500. It was decided to write off $28,500 of debts as irrecoverable. The allowance for receivables required was to be the equivalent of 5% of receivables.

What should be the charge in the statement of profit or loss for the year ended 30 September 20X3 for receivables expense?

A $42,000
B $33,925
C $70,500
D $32,500

The following information relates to questions 13 to 15

The total amount owed to Robert by his customers at 30 November 20X7 was $78,600.

His receivables allowance at 1 December 20X6 was $1,200.

On 30 November 20X7, Robert determined that a balance of $600 should be written off as irrecoverable. This amount has not been included in the receivables allowance. He also determined that an allowance equal to $1\frac{1}{2}$% of the remaining receivables balance should be made. Robert also received cash of $100 for a debt that was previously written off

13   Robert has made the entry in the receivables expense account to write off the irrecoverable balance.

What other entry does he need to make?

A   A debit entry in the revenue account
B   A credit entry in the revenue account
C   A debit entry in the receivables account
D   A credit entry in the receivables account

14   A company has received cash for a debt that was previously written off.

Which of the following is the correct double entry to record the cash received?

	Debit	Credit
A	Irrecoverable debts expense	Accounts receivable
B	Cash and bank	Irrecoverable debts expense
C	Allowance for receivables	Accounts receivable
D	Cash and bank	Allowance for receivables

15   How should the movement in the receivables allowance be reflected in the statement of profit or loss?

A   A credit of $21
B   A charge of $21
C   A credit of $30
D   A charge of $30

10 Accruals (and prepayments)

1   The annual insurance premium for S for the period 1 July 20X1 to 30 June 20X2 is $13,200, which is 10% more than the previous year. Insurance premiums are paid on 1 July.

What is the statement of profit or loss charge for the year ended 31 December 20X1?

A $11,800
B $12,540
C $12,600
D $13,200

2   The electricity account for the year ended 30 June 20X1 was as follows.

	$
Opening balance for electricity accrued at 1 July 20X0	300
Payments made during the year	
Bill dated 1 August 20X0 for three months to 31 July 20X0	600
Bill dated 1 November 20X0 for three months to 31 October 20X0	720
Bill dated 1 February 20X1 for three months to 31 January 20X1	900
Bill dated 30 June 20X1 for three months to 30 April 20X1	840

Which of the following is the appropriate entry for electricity?

	Accrued at 30 June 20X1	Charge to statement of profit or loss year ended 30 June 20X1
A	$Nil	$3,060
B	$460	$3,320
C	$560	$3,320
D	$560	$3,420

3   LH business rents out office space to MN at an annual rent of $48,000. MN makes payments one month in advance on the 1st of each month. All rental income has been received during the year ended 31 July 20X4.

Which of the following journal in respect of rental income should be recorded at 31 July 20X4?

A   Dr rental income $4,000; Cr current liabilities $4,000
B   Dr rental income $4,000; Cr prepayments $4,000
C   Dr prepayments $4,000; Cr rental income $4,000
D   Dr current liabilities $4,000; Cr rental income $4,000

---

4   D is preparing the accounts for A for the year ended 31 March 20X3. The most recent gas bill received by A was dated 6 February 20X3 and related to the quarter 1 November 20X2 to 31 January 20X3, and the amount of the bill was $2,100.

Which ONE of the following ledger entries should be made in A's books at 31 March 20X3?

		Debit		Credit
A	Accruals	Nil	Gas expense	Nil
B	Gas expense	$1,400	Accruals	$1,400
C	Accruals	$1,400	Gas expense	$1,400
D	Gas expense	$2,100	Accruals	$2,100

---

5   A company pays rent quarterly in arrears on 1 January, 1 April, 1 July and 1 October each year. The rent was increased from $90,000 per year to $120,000 per year, starting from 1 October 20X2.

What rent expense and accrual should be included in the company's financial statements for the year ended 31 January 20X3?

	Rent expense	Accrual
	$	$
A	100,000	20,000
B	100,000	10,000
C	97,500	10,000
D	97,500	20,000

---

6   Diesel fuel in inventory at 1 November 20X7 was $12,500, and there were invoices awaited for $1,700. During the year to 31 October 20X8, diesel fuel bills of $85,400 were paid, and a delivery worth $1,300 had yet to be invoiced. At 31 October 20X8, the inventory of diesel fuel was valued at $9,800.

The diesel fuel to be charged to the statement of profit or loss for the year to 31 October 20X8 is
$_____ .

---

7   A company's telephone bill consists of two elements. One is a quarterly rental charge, payable in advance; the other is a quarterly charge for calls made, payable in arrears. At 1 April 20X7, the previous bill dated 1 March 20X7 had included line rental of $90. Estimated call charges during March 20X7 were $80.

During the following 12 months, bills totalling $2,145 were received on 1 June, 1 September, 1 December 20X9 and 1 March 20X8, each containing rental of $90 as well as call charges. Estimated call charges for March 20X8 were $120.

The amount to be charged to the statement of profit or loss for the year ended 31 March 20X8 is
$_____ .

8   Business rates are paid annually on 1 April, to cover the following 12 months. The business rates for 20X1/X2 are $1,800, and for 20X2/20X3 are increased by 20%.

The charge for business rates in the statement of profit or loss for the year ended 30 April 20X2 is
$ _____ .

9   Rent is paid quarterly on the first day of May, August, November and February, in arrears. The rent has been $1,200 per annum for some time, but increases to $1,600 per annum from 1 February 20X2.

The charge for rent in the statement of profit or loss for the year ended 30 April 20X2 is
$ _____ .

10   The accountant at S is preparing quarterly accounts for Quarter 3. In Quarter 2, he had accrued $1,600 for gas and this balance was carried forward to Quarter 3. In Quarter 3, a gas bill of $2,700 was paid. The accountant has accrued $2,400 for gas in Quarter 3.

What should be the charge for gas in the statement of profit or loss for Quarter 3?

A $1,900
B $2,400
C $2,700
D $3,500

11   H began trading on 1 July 20X1. The company is now preparing its accounts for the accounting year ended 30 June 20X2. Rent is charged for a tax year, which runs from 1 April to 31 March, and was $1,800 for the year ended 31 March 20X2 and $2,000 for the year ended 31 March 20X3. Rent is payable quarterly in advance, plus any arrears, on 1 March, 1 June, 1 September and 1 December.

The charge to H's statement of profit or loss for rent for the year ended 30 June 20X2 is _____ .

12   The following totals appear in the day books for March 20X8.

	Goods excluding Sales tax	Sales tax
	$	$
Sales day book	40,000	7,000
Purchases day book	20,000	3,500
Returns inwards day book	2,000	350
Returns outward day book	4,000	700

Opening and closing inventories are both $3,000.

The gross profit for March 20X8 is _____

The following data relates to questions 13 to15.

At 1 October 20X5, the following balances were brought forward in the ledger accounts of XY:

Rent payable account	Dr	$1,000
Electricity account	Cr	$800
Interest receivable account	Dr	$300

You are told the following.

(a) Rent is payable quarterly in advance on the last day of November, February, May and August, at the rate of $6,000 per annum.

(b) Electricity is paid as follows.

5 November 20X5 $1,000 (for the period to 31 October 20X5)
10 February 20X6 $1,300 (for the period to 31 January 20X6)
8 May 20X6 $1,500 (for the period to 30 April 20X6)
7 August 20X6 $1,100 (for the period to 31 July 20X6)

At 30 September 20X6, the electricity meter shows that $900 has been consumed since the last bill was received.

(c) Interest was received during the year as follows.

2 October 20X5 $250 (for the six months to 30 September 20X5)
3 April 20X6 $600 (for the six months to 31 March 20X6)

You estimate that interest of $300 is accrued at 30 September 20X6.

13 The rent charge to the statement of profit or loss for the year is $ _____ .

14 The charge for electricity to the statement of profit or loss for the year is $ _____ .

15 The amount of interest receivable to appear in the statement of profit or loss for the year is
$ _____ .

11 Accounting for sales tax

1 The following information relates to Eva Co's sales tax for the month of March 20X3:

	$
Sales (including sales tax)	109,250
Purchases (net of sales tax)	64,000

Sales tax is charged at a flat rate of 15%. Eva Co's sales tax control account showed an opening credit balance of $4,540 at the beginning of the month; and a closing debit balance of $2,720 at the end of the month.

What was the total sales tax paid to the tax authorities during the month of March 20X3?

A $6,470
B $11,910
C $14,047.50
D $13,162.17

2 Alana is not registered for sales tax purposes. She has recently received an invoice for goods for resale which cost $500 before sales tax, which is levied at 15%. The total value was therefore $575.

What is the correct entry to be made in Alana's general ledger in respect of the invoice?

A   DR Purchases $500, DR Sales tax $75, CR Payables $575
B   DR Purchases $575, CR Sales tax $75, CR Payables $500
C   DR Purchases $500, CR Payables $500
D   DR Purchases $575, CR Payables $575

3   A sales tax registered business sells goods for $200 plus sales tax at 17.5% on credit. Which of the following entries correctly records this transaction?

    A   Debit   Sales ledger control account $235
            Credit Sales $235

    B   Debit   Sales ledger control account $200
            Credit Sales $165
            Credit Sales tax control account $35

    C   Debit   Sales ledger control account $235
            Credit Sales $200
            Credit Sales tax control account $35

    D   Debit   Sales $200
            Debit   Sales tax control account $35
            Credit Purchase ledger control account $235

4   A business commenced with capital in cash of $1,000. Inventory costing $800 plus sales tax is purchased on credit, and half is sold for $1,000 plus sales tax, the customer paying in cash at once. The sales tax rate is 20%.

    What would the accounting equation after these transactions show?

    A   Assets $1,800 less Liabilities $200 equals Capital $1,600
    B   Assets $2,200 less Liabilities $1,000 equals Capital $1,200
    C   Assets $2,600 less Liabilities $800 equals Capital $1,800
    D   Assets $2,600 less Liabilities $1,000 equals Capital $1,600

5   Trade receivables and payables in the final accounts of a sales tax registered trader will appear as described by which of the following?

    A   Inclusive of sales tax in the statement of financial position

    B   Exclusive of sales tax in the statement of financial position

    C   The sales tax is deducted and added to the sales tax account in the statement of financial position

    D   Sales tax does not appear in the statement of financial position because the business simply acts as a collector on behalf of the tax authorities

6   Persian Limited sells goods which are zero rated and standard rated for sales tax purposes.

    Tabby Co sells goods which are exempt from sales tax.

    Manx Brothers sells goods which are standard rated for sales tax purposes.

    Which of these entities can reclaim any input sales tax?

    A   Persian Limited only
    B   Persian Limited and Tabby Co
    C   Persian Limited and Manx Brothers
    D   Tabby Co and Manx Brothers

7   In the quarter ended 31 March 20X2, C had sales taxable outputs, net of sales tax, of $90,000 and taxable inputs, net of sales tax, of $72,000.

If the rate of sales tax is 10%, how much sales tax is due?

A $1,800 receivable
B $2,000 receivable
C $1,800 payable
D $2,000 payable

8   In July 20X2, a company sold goods at the standard sales tax rate with a net value of $200,000, goods exempt from sales tax with a value of $50,000 and goods at zero sales tax rate with a net value of $25,000. The purchases in July 20X2, which were all subject to sales tax, were $161,000, including sales tax. Assume that the rate of sales tax is 15%.

The difference between sales input tax and sales output tax is:

A   DR $9,000
B   CR $5,850
C   CR $9,000
D   DR $5,850

9   N, which is registered for sales tax, received an invoice from an advertising agency for $4,000 plus sales tax. The rate of sales tax on the goods was 17.5%. The correct ledger entries are:

	Debit	$	Credit	$
A	Advertising expense	4,000	Payables	4,000
B	Advertising expense	4,700	Payables	4,700
C	Advertising expense	4,700	Payables	4,000
			Sales tax control account	700
D	Advertising expense	4,000	Payables	4,700
	Sales tax control account	700		

10   W is registered for sales tax. The managing director has asked four staff in the accounts department why the output tax for the last quarter does not equal 20% of sales (20% is the rate of tax).

Which one of the following four replies that she received was not correct?

A   The company had some exports that were not liable for sales tax
B   The company made some sales of zero-rated products
C   The company made some sales of exempt products
D   The company sold some products to businesses not registered for sales tax

11   Which of the following correctly describe the entry in the sales account for a sale for a sales tax registered trader?

A   Credited with the total of sales made, including sales tax
B   Credited with the total of sales made, excluding sales tax
C   Debited with the total of sales made, including sales tax
D   Debited with the total of sales made, excluding sales tax

12 Sales (including sales tax) amounted to $27,612.50, and purchases (excluding sales tax) amounted to $18,000. What is the balance on the sales tax control account, assuming all items are subject to sales tax at 17.5%?

A $962.50 debit
B $962.50 credit
C $1,682.10 debit
D $1,682.10 credit

The following data relates to questions 13 to 15.

Your organisation has recently employed a new accounts assistant who is unsure about the correct use of books of original entry and the need for adjustments to be made to the accounts at the end of the year. You have been asked to give the new assistant some guidance.

For each of the following examples of transactions to be recorded in the books of original entry, complete the double entry posting sheet below.

13   Purchase of raw materials on credit from J Burgess, list price $27,000 less trade discount of $33^1/_3$%, plus sales tax of 17.5%.

14   Returns of goods sold to J Lockley, total invoice value of $470, including sales tax of 17.5%.

15   A credit note from supplier AS Supplies for inferior materials returned. The net amount is $480, with sales tax of 17.5%.

DOUBLE ENTRY POSTING SHEET

ITEM	BOOK OF ORIGINAL ENTRY	DEBIT ENTRIES Account	$	CREDIT ENTRIES Account	$
Question 13 (i)					
Question 14 (ii)					
Question 15 (iii)					

12 Accounting for payroll

1   A business paid out $15,000 in net wages to its employees. In respect of these wages, the following amounts were shown in the statement of financial position.

	$
Income tax payable	3,000
National Insurance payable – employees'	1,650
– employer's	1,800
Pension payable for employees' contributions	1,050

Employees' gross wages, before deductions, were?

A $20,700
B $19,650
C $22,500
D $18,000

2   An employee has a gross weekly wage of $440.00. For this week, his income tax payable through the PAYE system is $77.76. The employees' NIC for the week is $43.18 and 5% of his gross wage is deducted each week as a pension contribution. The employer's NIC for the week is $49.35.

What is the employees' net wage for the week?

A $362.24
B $247.71
C $297.06
D $303.11

---

3   Double entry for payment of net wages is:

A	Debit	Wages and salaries expense	Credit Bank
B	Debit	Bank	Credit Wages control
C	Debit	Wages and salaries expense	Credit Wages control
D	Debit	Wages control	Credit Bank

---

4   You have obtained the following information from PY's payroll records relating to one of its employees:

Gross monthly salary	$2,500
Employee income tax rate	20%
Employee social security contributions	5%
Employer social security contributions	10%

What is the annual cost to PY of employing this member of staff?

$_____

---

5   Paul paid $240,000 in net wages to its employees in August 20X2. Employees' tax was $24,000, employees' national insurance was $12,000 and employer's national insurance was $14,000. Employees had contributed $6,000 to a pension scheme and had voluntarily asked for $3,000 to be deducted for charitable giving.

The amount to be charged to the statement of profit or loss in August 20X2 for wages is:

A $296,000
B $299,000
C $290,000
D $264,000

---

6   An employee is paid at the rate of $3.50 per hour. Earnings of more than $75 a week are taxed at 20%. Employees' National Insurance is 7%, and Employer's National Insurance is 10%. During week 24, the employee works for 36 hours.

The amounts to be charged to the statement of profit or loss and paid to the employee are:

Statement of profit or loss   Paid to employee

_____   _____

7   The total cost of salaries charged to a limited liability company's statement of profit or loss is:

A   Cash paid to employees
B   Net pay earned by employees
C   Gross pay earned by employees
D   Gross pay earned by employees, plus employer's national insurance contributions

8   A business paid out $12,450 in net wages to its employees. In respect of these wages, the following amounts were shown in the statement of financial position.

	$
Income tax payable	2,480
National Insurance payable – employees'	1,350
– employer's	1,500

No other deductions were made.

Employees' gross wages, before deductions, were:

A $12,450
B $27,450
C $16,280
D $17,780

9   The following data has been extracted from the payroll records of Kleen Ltd for the month of February 20X1.

	$
Income tax	17,000
Employer's NIC	7,500
Employees' NIC	6,000
Cash paid to employees	50,000

The wage expense for the month is:

A $50,000
B $56,000
C $74,500
D $80,500

10   An employee has a gross monthly salary of $1,500. In September, the tax deducted was $300, the employee's national insurance was $90, and the employer's national insurance was $150.

What was the charge for wages and salaries in the statement of profit or loss?

A $1,110
B $1,410
C $1,500
D $1,650

11 Gross wages paid should be debited to?

    A   Debited to SPL as the total wages and salaries expense

    B   Debited to wages control account

    C   Debited to bank account

    D   Debited to Sundry expenses

12 The following details have been extracted from the payroll records for the month of May:

	$
Gross wages	25,500
Employer's benefit contribution	1,800
Employer's pension contribution	1,200

What is the correct journal for posting these details to the ledger accounts?

		$	$
A	DR Staff costs	28,500	
	CR Wages control		28,500
B	DR Staff costs	27,300	
	CR Wages control		27,300
C	DR Staff costs	26,700	
	CR Wages control		26,700
D	DR Staff costs	25,500	
	CR Wages control		25,500

The following data relates to questions 13 to 15

You are an accounts assistant at Klemspeck Supplies Ltd. You have been given the following payroll figures for December 20X6 from the payroll officer.

	$
Gross pay	10,329
Employee's national insurance	626
Employer's national insurance	1,054
Employee's pension deductions	546
Employer's contribution to pension	721
Income tax	2,114

Employees are paid for the month worked, at the end of that month.

Payments of tax, national insurance and pension contributions are made one months in arrears.

13 What is the net pay figure for April 20X6?

    Net pay is _____ .

14 What is the total payroll cost in the statement of profit or loss for December 20X6?

    Total payroll cost is _____ .

15   What is the correct journal entry to record payments due for national insurance for the month of December 20X6?

A   DEBIT   NIC control account   Employee national insurance deduction
     DEBIT   Wages control account   Employer's national insurance

B   DEBIT   Wages control account   Employee national insurance deduction
     CREDIT   NIC control account   Employee national insurance deduction

C   DEBIT   Wages control account   Employee national insurance deduction
     CREDIT   NIC control account   Employee national insurance deduction
     DEBIT   Employer's NIC (SPL)   Employer's national insurance
     CREDIT   NIC control account   Employer's national insurance

D   DEBIT   NIC control account   Employee national insurance deduction
     CREDIT   Wages control account   Employee national insurance deduction
     DEBIT   NIC control account   Employer's national insurance
     CREDIT   Employer's NIC (SPL)   Employer's national insurance

13 Bank reconciliations

1   When preparing a bank reconciliation, it is realised that:

(i)   Cheques with a value of $1,050 have been sent to suppliers and correctly entered in the cash book, but have not yet been presented for payment.

(ii)   A cheque for $75 sent to a supplier has been incorrectly recorded in the cash book as $57.

(iii) Before correction, the cash book has a balance of $10,500 credit.

(iv)   Bank charges of $175 have not been recorded in the cash book.

What is the closing balance shown on the bank statement?

A $9,257 overdrawn
B $9,643 overdrawn
C $11,357 overdrawn
D $11,743 overdrawn

2   A company has an opening cash book balance of $5,000 debit. During the month, the company received $26,000 from receivables, cash sales were $2,500 and payments were made to payables of $12,000 less 2% cash discounts. A comparison with the bank statement showed $125 bank charges had not been recorded in the cash book. What is the adjusted cash book balance?

A $21,855 credit
B $21,615 debit
C $21,375 debit
D $18,875 credit

3   Your cash book at 31 December 20X3 shows a bank balance of $565 overdrawn. On comparing this with your bank statement at the same date, you discover the following.

1   A cheque for $57 drawn by you on 29 December 20X3 has not yet been presented for payment.

2   A cheque for $92 from a customer, which was paid into the bank on 24 December 20X3, has been dishonoured on 31 December 20X3.

What is the correct bank balance to be shown in the statement of financial position at 31 December 20X3?

A $714 overdrawn
B $657 overdrawn
C $473 overdrawn
D $53 overdrawn

4   Your firm's cash book at 30 April 20X8 shows a balance at the bank of $2,490. Comparison with the bank statement at the same date reveals the following differences:

	$
Unpresented cheques	840
Bank charges not in cash book	50
Receipts not yet credited by the bank	470

It has transpired that a cheque from a customer previously entered in the cashbook has been dishonoured at the bank to the value of $140. What is the adjusted bank balance per the cash book at 30 April 20X8?

A $1,460
B $2,300
C $2,580
D $3,140

5   Listed below are some possible causes of difference between the cash book balance and the bank statement balance when preparing a bank reconciliation:

1   Cheque paid in, subsequently dishonoured
2   Error by bank
3   Bank charges
4   Lodgements credited after date
5   Outstanding cheques not yet presented

Which of these items require an entry in the cash book?

A   1 and 3 only
B   1, 2, 3, 4 and 5
C   2, 4, and 5 only
D   4 and 5 only

6   When preparing a bank reconciliation, it is realised that:

    1   There are unpresented cheques of $8,000
    2   There are lodgements of $5,000 uncleared
    3   Bank charges of $67 have not been recorded in the cash book

    What adjustment is required to the cash account?

    A   Debit $67
    B   Credit $67
    C   Debit $3,067
    D   Credit $3,067

---

7   A business has the following cash and bank transactions during January 20X1. Balance 1.1.20X1: cash $500, bank $1,000 overdrawn, receipts of cash $12,600, cash paid $3,200, cash paid to bank $5,500, payments by cheque $8,200. Closing balances: cash $600, bank $6,200 overdrawn.

    Calculate the total cash and bank drawings.

    A $14,800 (no bank drawings)
    B $860
    C $11,800
    D $6,300

---

8   Sandiland's cash book for the month of May 20X3 was extracted on 31 May and is summarised below.

	$		$
Opening balance	546	Payments	335,966
Receipts	336,293	Closing balance	873
	336,839		336,839

    The company's financial controller provides you with the following information.

    (a)   The company's bank statement for May was received on 1 June and showed an overdrawn balance of $1,444 at the end of May.

    (b)   Cheques paid to various payables totalling $7,470 have not yet been presented to the bank.

    (c)   Cheques received by Sandilands totalling $6,816 were paid into the bank on 31 May but not credited by the bank until 2 June.

    (d)   Bank charges of $630 shown on the bank statement have not been entered in the company's cash book.

    (e)   Direct debits entered on the bank statement totalling $2,584 have not been recorded in the company's cash book.

    (f)   A cheque drawn by Sandilands for $693 and presented to the bank on 26 May has been incorrectly entered in the cash book as $936.

    The corrected cash book balance at 31 May is $ _____ .

9   At 31 December 20X9, the cash book of a company shows a credit balance of $901. When the bank statement for the month of December was compared with the cash book, it was discovered that cheques totalling $2,468 had been drawn but not presented to the bank, and cheques received totalling $593 had not yet been credited by the bank.

The balance on the bank statement at 31 December 20X9 was _____ .

10   Your firm's bank statement at 31 October 20X8 shows a balance of $13,400. You subsequently discover that the bank has dishonoured a customer's cheque for $300 and has charged bank charges of $50, neither of which is recorded in your cash book. There are unpresented cheques totalling $2,400. Amounts paid in, but not yet credited by the bank, amount to $1,000. You further discover that an automatic receipt from a customer of $195 has been recorded as a credit in your cash book.

Your cash book balance, prior to correcting the errors and omissions, was:

A $11,455
B $11,960
C $12,000
D $12,155

11   The bank statement at 31 December 20X1 shows a balance of $1,000. The cash book shows a balance of $750 in hand.

Which of the following is the most likely reason for the difference?

A   Receipts of $250 recorded in cash book, but not yet recorded by bank
B   Bank charges of $250 shown on the bank statement, not in the cash book
C   Standing orders of $250 included on bank statement, not in the cash book
D   Cheques for $250 recorded in the cash book, but not yet gone through the bank account

12   When preparing a bank reconciliation it is realised that:

1   Cheques with a value of $1,050 have been sent to suppliers and correctly entered in the cash book, but have not yet been presented for payment.

2   A cheque for $75 sent to a supplier has been incorrectly recorded in the cash book as $57.

3   Before correction, the cash book has a balance of $10,500 credit.

4   Bank charges of $175 have not been recorded in the cash book.

The balance of the cashbook after the correction is:

A $10,307 overdrawn
B $10,343 overdrawn
C $10,657 overdrawn
D $10,693 overdrawn

The following information if relevant to questions 13 to 15

On 10 January 20X9, Jane Smith received her monthly bank statement for December 20X8. The statement showed the following.

SOUTHERN BANK PLC

Date	Particulars	Debits	Credits	Balance
20X8		$	$	$
Dec 1	Balance			1,862
Dec 5	417864	243		1,619
Dec 5	Dividend		26	1,645
Dec 5	Bank Credit		212	1,857
Dec 8	417866	174		1,683
Dec 10	417867	17		1,666
Dec 11	Sundry Credit		185	1,851
Dec 14	Standing Order	32		1,819
Dec 20	417865	307		1,512
Dec 20	Bank Credit		118	1,630
Dec 21	417868	95		1,535
Dec 21	417870	161		1,374
Dec 24	Bank charges	18		1,356
Dec 27	Bank Credit		47	1,403
Dec 28	Direct Debit	88		1,315
Dec 29	417873	12		1,303
Dec 29	Bank Credit		279	1,582
Dec 31	417871	25		1,557

Her cash book for the corresponding period showed:

CASH BOOK

20X8		$	20X8		Cheque no	$
Dec 1	Balance b/d	1,862	Dec 1	Electricity	864	243
Dec 4	J Shannon	212	Dec 2	P Simpson	865	307
Dec 9	M Lipton	185	Dec 5	D Underhill	866	174
Dec 19	G Hurst	118	Dec 6	A Young	867	17
Dec 26	M Evans	47	Dec 10	T Unwin	868	95
Dec 27	J Smith	279	Dec 14	B Oliver	869	71
Dec 29	V Owen	98	Dec 16	Rent	870	161
Dec 30	K Walters	134	Dec 20	M Peters	871	25
			Dec 21	L Philips	872	37
			Dec 22	W Hamilton	873	12
			Dec 31	Balance c/d		1,793
		2,935				2,935

13   What is the purpose of Jane carrying out a bank reconciliation?

A   To enable the bank to decide whether to make a loan to a business

B   To discover whether the bank has been over-charging its customers

C   To identify and account for the differences between the general ledger bank account and the bank statement

D   To ensure that the total on the general ledger bank account is exactly the same as that on the bank statement

14   Calculate the corrected cash book balance as at 31 December 20X8:

_____

15   Fill in the missing words and figures.

To reconcile the balance per the bank statement at 31 December 20X8 with the corrected cashbook balance at that date:

- Add _____ of $ _____ ; and
- Deduct _____ of $ _____

14 Control accounts

1   A supplier sends you a statement showing a balance outstanding of $14,350. Your own records show a balance outstanding of $14,500.

The reason for this difference could be that:

A   The supplier sent an invoice for $150 which you have not yet received
B   The supplier has allowed you $150 cash discount which you had omitted to enter in your ledgers
C   You have paid the supplier $150 which he has not yet accounted for
D   You have returned goods worth $150 which the supplier has not yet accounted for

2   Which of the following is NOT the purpose of a receivables control account?

A   A receivables control account provides a check on the arithmetical accuracy of the personal ledger
B   A receivables control account helps to locate errors in the trial balance
C   A receivables control account ensures that there are no errors in the personal ledger
D   Control accounts deter fraud

3   When reconciling the list of receivables to the receivables control account, it is discovered that:

(i)   A credit balance of $150 on a customer's account has been treated as a debit balance
(ii)   A debit balance of $120 on a customer's account has been omitted

What is the required adjustment to the list of balances?

A   Add $30
B   Subtract $30
C   Add $180
D   Subtract $180

4   When reconciling the receivables control account to the list of balances, it was discovered that the sales daybook has been overcast by $50.

What adjustment is necessary to the list of balances?

A   No adjustment
B   Add $50
C   Subtract $50
D   Subtract $100

5   When reconciling the receivables control account to the list of balances, it is discovered that $2,000 of goods returned by customers were not recorded in the nominal ledger.

What is the required adjustment to the receivables control account?

A   Debit $2,000
B   Credit $2,000
C   Debit $4,000
D   Credit $4,000

6   Your organisation sold goods to PQ for $800 less trade discount of 20% and cash discount of 5% for payment within 14 days. The invoice was settled by cheque five days later. What is the double entry for the cash discount allowed?

Debit	Credit
$	$
_____	_____

7   A receivables control account showed a debit balance of $37,642. The individual receivables' accounts in the sales ledger showed a total of $35,840. The difference could be due to entering discount allowed of _____ on the debit side of the control account.

8   A debit balance of $1,250 on X's account in the books of Y means that:

X _____ Y

9   A business has the following transactions for the month of June 20X2:

Credit sales	164,500
Sales returns	6,200
Cheques from receivables	155,300
Discounts allowed to customers	5,100
Irrecoverable debt written off	2,600

The receivables balance at 30 June 20X2 was $8,300.

The receivables balance at 1 June 20X2 was $ _____ .

10   The receivables control account at 1 May had balances of $32,750 debit and $1,275 credit. During May, sales of $125,000 were made on credit. Receipts from receivables amounted to $122,500 and cash discounts of $550 were allowed. Refunds of $1,300 were made to customers.

The closing balances at 31 May could be:

A $35,175 debit and $3,000 credit
B $35,675 debit and $2,500 credit
C $36,725 debit and $2,000 credit
D $36,725 debit and $1,000 credit

---

11   The total of the balances in the payables control account is $1,500 more than the total of the payable balances extracted from the purchase ledger.

Which of the following would explain this difference?

A   The purchase day book is overcast by $1,500

B   Discounts received have not been posted in the purchase ledger accounts

C   Cash paid to payables has not been posted in some accounts in the purchase ledger

D   A contra entry between the purchase and sales ledgers has been omitted from the purchase ledger but was posted in the control account

---

12   When reconciling control accounts to lists of balances, a casting error in a daybook will require adjustments:

A   To both the control account and the list of balances
B   To neither the control account nor the list of balances
C   To the control account, but not the list of balances
D   To the list of balances, but not the control account

The following scenario relates to questions 13 to 15.

P & Co maintain a receivables ledger control account within the nominal ledger. At 30 November 20X0, the total of the list of individual balances extracted from the receivables ledger was $15,800, which did not agree with the balance on the receivables ledger control account. An examination of the books revealed the following information, which can be used to reconcile the receivables ledger and the receivables ledger control account.

1   The credit balance of $420 in Ahmed's payables ledger account had been set off against his account in the receivables ledger, but no entries had been made in the receivables and payables ledger control accounts.

2   The personal account of Mahmood was undercast by $90.

3   Yasmin's balance of (debit) $780 had been omitted from the list of balances.

4   Thomas' personal account balance of $240 had been removed from the receivables ledger as an irrecoverable debt, but no entry had been made in the receivables ledger control account.

5   The January total of $8,900 in the sales daybook had been posted as $9,800.

6   A credit note to Charles for $1,000, plus sales tax of $300, had been posted to the receivables ledger control account as $1,300 and to Charles' personal account as $1,000.

7   The total on the credit side of Edward's personal account had been overcast by $125.

13   Which of these items need to be corrected by journal entries in the nominal ledger?

  A   1, 3, 4 and 5 only
  B   1, 4 and 5 only
  C   1, 2, 5 and 6 only
  D   2, 3, 6 and 7 only

14   What is the revised total of the balances in the receivables ledger after the errors have been corrected?

  A $15,105
  B $16,195
  C $16,495
  D $16,915

15   Assuming that the closing balance on the receivables ledger control account should be $16,000, what is the opening balance on the receivables ledger control account before the errors were corrected?

  A $14,440
  B $15,760
  C $17,560
  D $17,860

15 Correction of errors

1   A suspense account was opened when a trial balance failed to agree. The following errors were later discovered.

  •   A gas bill of $420 had been recorded in the gas account as $240
  •   A discount of $50 given to a customer had been credited to discounts received
  •   Interest received of $70 had been entered in the bank account only

The original balance on the suspense account was:

  A   Debit $210
  B   Credit $210
  C   Debit $160
  D   Credit $160

2   An error of commission is one where:

  A   A transaction has not been recorded

  B   One side of a transaction has been recorded in the wrong class of account, such as non-current assets posted to inventory

  C   An error has been made in posting a transaction

  D   The digits in a number are recorded the wrong way round

3   Where a transaction is entered into the correct ledger accounts, but the wrong amount is used, the error is known as an error of:

    A   Omission
    B   Original entry
    C   Commission
    D   Principle

4   Which ONE of the following is an error of principle?

    A   A gas bill credited to the gas account and debited to the bank account

    B   The purchase of a non-current asset credited to the asset account at cost and debited to the payable's account

    C   The purchase of a non-current asset debited to the purchases account and credited to the payable's account

    D   The payment of wages debited and credited to the correct accounts, but using the wrong amount

5   When a trial balance was prepared, the closing inventory of $20,400 was omitted. To make the trial balance, a suspense account was opened.

What was the balance on the suspense account?

    A   Nil
    B   Debit $20,400
    C   Credit $20,400
    D   Debit $40,800

6   It has been discovered that the opening inventory figure of $1,000 has been omitted from the trial balance. A suspense account has been created as a result of this omission.

What was the balance on the suspense account?

    A   Nil
    B   Debit $1,000
    C   Credit $1,000
    D   Debit $2,000

7   Some inventory taken by the owner of a business has not yet been recorded. When this transaction is recorded:

    A   Profit will rise and net assets fall
    B   Profit will rise and net assets stay the same
    C   Profit will fall and net assets rise
    D   Profit will fall and net assets stay the same

8   Materials used to improve some machinery have been treated as purchases in the draft accounts. The necessary correction will:

A   Increase both profit and net assets
B   Increase profit and reduce net assets
C   Reduce profit and increase net assets
D   Reduce both profit and net assets

9   A loan repayable in 16 months has been included in current liabilities in the draft statement of financial position.

The necessary adjustment will:

A   Increase both current assets and net assets
B   Increase current assets and reduce net assets
C   Reduce current assets and increase net assets
D   Increase net current assets but leave net assets unchanged

10 It is realised that inventory which cost $5,000 with a net realisable value of $6,000 was excluded from a inventory take. The correction of this omission causes profit to:

A   Fall by $1,000
B   Rise by $1,000
C   Fall by $5,000
D   Rise by $5,000

11 Following the preparation of the statement of profit or loss, it is discovered that accrued expenses of $1,000 have been ignored and that closing inventory has been overvalued by $1,300. This will have resulted in:

A   An overstatement of net profit of $300
B   An understatement of net profit of $300
C   An overstatement of net profit of $2,300
D   An understatement of net profit of $2,300

12 A trial balance has failed to agree. The totals of the debits amounted to $157,800, the credit balances totalled $155,300. The difference was posted to a suspense account.

Which of the following would explain this difference?

A   The payment of a rent expense was recorded as:
    Dr   Bank $2,500
    Cr   Rent $2,500

B   An invoice for advertising costs of $1,250 was debited to the advertising account and also debited to the bank account.

C   An invoice for the purchase of inventory was omitted from the accounts.

D   A sundry receipt of $1,250 was debited to income and credited to cash.

The following data relates to questions 13 to 15.

After calculating net profit for the year ended 31 March 20X8, WL has the following trial balance.

	DR $	CR $
Land and buildings – cost	10,000	
Land and buildings – depreciation at 31 March 20X8		2,000
Plant – cost	12,000	
Plant – depreciation at 31 March 20X8		3,000
Inventories	2,500	
Trade receivables	1,500	
Bank	8,250	
Trade payables		1,700
Rent prepaid	400	
Wages accrued		300
Capital account		19,400
Profit for the year ended 31 March 20X8		9,750
	34,650	36,150

A suspense account was opened for the difference in the trial balance.

Immediately after production of the above, the following errors were discovered:

(i)   A payables account had been debited with a $300 sales invoice (which had been correctly recorded in the sales account).

(ii) The heat and light account had been credited with gas paid $150.

(iii) G Gordon had been credited with a cheque received from G Goldman for $800. Both are trade receivables.

13   Prepare a journal entry to correct error (i).

	Debit $	Credit $
_____	_____	
_____		_____

14   Prepare a journal entry to correct error (ii).

	Debit $	Credit $
_____	_____	
_____		_____

15   Prepare a journal entry to correct error (iii).

	Debit $	Credit $
_____	_____	
_____		_____

16 Incomplete records

1   At 1/1/X1 receivables owed $3,050, and at 31/12/X1 they owed $4,000. Cash received from receivables during the year was $22,000 (including a previously written of debt of $1,000). All sales were made at a 20% gross profit margin and no inventory are held.

What were purchases for the year?

A $21,950
B $18,292
C $17,560
D $4,390

2   If the mark-up is 30% and the cost of sales is $28,000, and expenses are $14,000, what is the net profit?

A   Profit $2,000
B   Loss $2,000
C   Profit $5,600
D   Loss $5,600

3   If sales were $25,500, and cost of sales was $21,250, what was the gross profit percentage?

A   16.67%
B   20%
C   83.333%
D   120%

4   A sole trader has net assets of $19,000 at 30 April 20X1. During the year to 30 April 20X1, he introduced $9,800 additional capital into the business. Profits were $8,000, of which he withdrew $4,200. His capital at 1 May 20X0 was:

A $3,000
B $5,400
C $13,000
D $16,600

5   P is a sole proprietor whose accounting records are incomplete. All the sales are cash sales and during the year $50,000 was banked, including $5,000 from the sale of a business car. He paid $12,000 wages in cash from the till and withdrew $2,000 per month as drawings. The cash in the till at the beginning and end of the year was $300 and $400 respectively.

What were the sales for the year?

A $80,900
B $81,000
C $81,100
D $86,100

6   The debit side of a trial balance totals $50 more than the credit side. This could be due to:

   A   A purchase of goods for $50 being omitted from the payable's account
   B   A sale of goods for $50 being omitted from the receivable's account
   C   An invoice of $25 for electricity being credited to the electricity account
   D   A receipt for $50 from a receivable being omitted from the cash book

7   Opening inventory is $1,000, purchases are $10,000 and sales are $15,000. The gross profit margin is 30%.
   Closing inventory is $ _____ .

8   A business has $900 in the cash account at the start of the year and $680 at the end of the year.

   During the year, $3,550 was received into the cash account from cash sales and $2,400 was paid out in expenses.

   In addition, money has been paid from the cash account to the petty cash tin. However, a record has not been kept of the amount transferred to petty cash.

   How much has been transferred from the cash account to petty cash in the year?

   A $930
   B $1,150
   C $1,370
   D $2,730

9   At 31 December 20X1, a business had:

Vehicles	2,000
Inventory	500
Receivables	300
Accrued electricity expense	50
Rent prepaid	200

   At 31 December 20X2, it had:

Vehicles	2,500
Inventory	100
Receivables	50
Payables	600
Accrued electricity expense	100
Rent prepaid	250

   The owner has drawn $1,000 in cash over the year.

   What is the profit or loss?

   A   Loss $250
   B   Profit $250
   C   Loss $750
   D   Profit $750

10   Which statement is wrong for a statement of financial position to balance?

      A   Net assets = Proprietor's fund
      B   Net assets = Capital + profit + drawings
      C   Net assets = Capital + profit − drawings
      D   Non-current assets + net current assets = capital + profit − drawings

11   During the year, all sales were made at a gross profit margin of 15%. Sales were $25,500, purchases were $22,000 and closing inventory was $4,000.

      What was opening inventory?

      A $3,675
      B $4,000
      C $4,174
      D $4,325

12   During the year, all sales were made with a 20% mark-up on cost. Sales were $25,500, purchases were $26,000 and closing inventory was $10,000.

      What was opening inventory?

      A $4,150
      B $5,250
      C $10,000
      D $14,750

The following information is relevant for questions 13 to 15.

Anna is a sole trader who does not keep full accounting records. The following details relate to her transactions with credit customers and suppliers for the year ended 30 November 20X3.

	$
Trade receivables, 1 December 20X2	130,000
Trade payables, 1 December 20X2	60,000
Cash received from customers	686,400
Cash paid to suppliers	302,800
Discounts allowed	1,400
Discounts received	2,960
Irrecoverable debts	4,160
Amount due from a customer who is also a supplier offset against an amount due for goods supplied by them	2,000
Trade receivables, 30 November 20X3	181,000
Trade payables, 30 November 20X3	84,000

13   Which of the following calculations could produce an acceptable figure for Anna's net profit for the period if no accounting records had been kept?

      A   Closing net assets + drawings − capital introduced − opening net assets = Net profit
      B   Closing net assets − drawings + capital introduced − opening net assets = Net profit
      C   Closing net assets − drawings − capital introduced − opening net assets = Net profit
      D   Closing net assets + drawings + capital introduced − opening net assets = Net profit

BPP
LEARNING MEDIA

14   Based on the above information, what figure should appear in Anna's statement of profit or loss for the year ended 30 November 20X3 for sales revenue?

     A $748,960
     B $748,800
     C $744,960
     D $743,560

15   Based on the above information, what figure should appear in Anna's statement of profit or loss for the year ended 30 November 20X3 for purchases?

     A $283,760
     B $325,840
     C $329,760
     D $331,760

17 Limited company financial statements

1   Which of the following items would be classified under current assets in the statement of financial position of a company?

     1   Trade payables
     2   Inventories
     3   Prepaid expenses
     4   Bank overdraft
     5   Tax owed by the tax authorities

     A   1, 2 and 5
     B   2, 3 and 5
     C   1 and 4 only
     D   2 and 3 only

2   A company has made a revaluation gain on one of its properties during the year.

   Which THREE of the following statements are correct in relation to the revaluation gain?

     1   It will be reported in the statement of profit or loss.
     2   It will be reported in other comprehensive income for the year.
     3   It will be shown as a cash inflow in the cash flow statement.
     4   It will be reported in the statement of changes in equity
     5   It will increase the value of non-current assets in the statement of financial position.

     A   1, 3 and 5
     B   1 and 4
     C   2, 3 and 4
     D   2, 4 and 5

3   Which one of the following items does not appear under the equity heading on a company statement of financial position?

A   Share premium account
B   Retained earnings
C   Revaluation surplus
D   Loan stock

4   According IAS 1 *Presentation of financial statements*, where should dividends paid during the year be disclosed?

A   Statement of profit or loss and other comprehensive income

B   Statement of changes in equity

C   Statement of financial position

D   In both the statement of financial position and the statement of profit or loss and other comprehensive income.

5   A company has $500,000, 15% debentures which were originally issued at par. The company had paid interest half yearly but the final instalment is outstanding at the year end.

Which of the following statements is correct?

A   The interest charge in the statement of profit or loss account will be $75,000.
B   The interest charge in the statement of profit or loss account will be $37,500.
C   The statement of financial position will contain a liability for outstanding interest of $75,000.
D   The interest charge in the statement of profit or loss account will be $112,500.

6   Which of the following items may appear as current liabilities in a company's statement of financial position?

1   Revaluation surplus
2   Loan due for repayment within one year
3   Taxation
4   Accrued expenses

A   1, 2 and 3
B   1, 2 and 4
C   1, 3 and 4
D   2, 3 and 4

7   Distributable reserves would decrease if a company:

A   Sets aside profits to pay future dividends
B   Transfers amounts into 'general reserves'
C   Issues shares at a premium
D   Pays dividends

8   Which ONE of the following does NOT form part of the equity capital of a limited company?

    A   Non-current bank liabilities
    B   Share premium
    C   Revaluation surplus
    D   Ordinary share capital

9   A company has authorised capital of 50,000 5% preference shares of $2 each and 500,000 ordinary shares with a par value of 20c each. All of the preference shares have been issued. Only 400,000 ordinary shares have been issued; they were issued at a premium of 30c each. Interim dividends of 5c per ordinary share, plus half the preference dividend, have been paid during the current year. A final dividend of 15c per ordinary share is declared.

    The total of dividends payable for the year is:

    A $82,500
    B $85,000
    C $102,500
    D $105,000

10   In a set of company accounts, which would normally increase administration expenses?

    A   Reduction in the allowance for receivables
    B   Depreciation of machinery in the factory
    C   Accrual of the audit fee
    D   Payment of production director's salary

18 Issue of shares

1   At 30 June 20X2 a company's capital structure was as follows:

	$
Ordinary share capital	
500,000 shares of 25c each	125,000
Share premium account	100,000

    In the year ended 30 June 20X3, the company made a rights issue of 1 share for every 2 held at $1 per share and this was taken up in full. Later in the year, the company made a bonus issue of 1 share for every 5 held, using the share premium account for the purpose.

    What was the company's capital structure at 30 June 20X3?

	Ordinary share capital	Share premium account
	$	$
A	450,000	25,000
B	225,000	250,000
C	225,000	325,000
D	212,500	262,500

2   A limited liability company issued 50,000 ordinary shares of 25c each at a premium of 50c per share. The cash received was correctly recorded but the full amount was credited to the ordinary share capital account.

Which one of the following journal entries is needed to correct this error?

		Debit $	Credit $
A	Share premium account	25,000	
	Share capital account		25,000
B	Share capital account	25,000	
	Share premium account		25,000
C	Share capital account	37,500	
	Share premium account		37,500
D	Share capital account	25,000	
	Cash and bank		25,000

3   The correct ledger entries needed to record the issue of 200,000 $1 shares at a premium of 30c, and paid for in full, would be:

A	Dr Ordinary share capital	$200,000	
	Cr Share premium account		$60,000
	Cr Cash		$140,000
B	Dr Cash	$260,000	
	Cr Ordinary share capital		$200,000
	Cr Share premium account		$60,000
C	Dr Ordinary share capital	$200,000	
	Dr Share premium account	$60,000	
	Cr Cash		$260,000
D	Dr Cash	$200,000	
	Dr Share premium account	$60,000	
	Cr Ordinary share capital		$260,000

4   At 1 January 20X0, the capital structure of Q, a limited liability company, was as follows:

	$
Issued share capital 1,000,000 ordinary shares of 50c each	500,000
Share premium account	300,000

On 1 April 20X0, the company made an issue of 200,000 50c shares at $1.30 each, and on 1 July, the company made a bonus (capitalisation) issue of one share for every four in issue at the time, using the share premium account for the purpose.

Which of the following correctly states the company's share capital and share premium account at 31 December 20X0?

	Share capital	Share premium account
A	$750,000	$230,000
B	$875,000	$285,000
C	$750,000	$310,000
D	$750,000	$610,000

5   When a company makes a rights issue of equity shares, which of the following effects will the issue have?

1   Assets are increased
2   Retained earnings are reduced
3   Share premium account is reduced
4   Investments are increased

A   1 only
B   1 and 2
C   3 only
D   1 and 4

6   Which THREE of the following statements are true in respect of a rights issue of shares?

1   The share capital account will increase and the share premium account will decrease.

2   The share capital account will increase and the share premium account will increase.

3   The share capital account will be credited with the issue price of the share.

4   The share capital account will be credited with the nominal value of the share and any excess between the issue price and nominal value will be credited to the share premium account.

5   The total proceeds received from the rights issue will be shown in the statement of changes in equity.

6   Only the nominal value of the shares will be shown in the statement of changes in equity.

A   1, 3 and 6
B   3 and 4
C   1, 2 and 4
D   2, 4 and 5

7   'When a company makes a bonus issue of shares, this raises additional finance.'

Is this statement true or false?

A   True
B   False

The following data relates to questions 8 to 10

Given below are extracts from the trial balance of FG at 31 March 20X2 after preparation of the draft statement of profit or loss.

	$
Share capital (50 cents ordinary shares)	200,000
Share premium account	40,000
General reserve	20,000
Retained earnings at 31 March 20X2	84,000

Since preparation of the draft statement of profit or loss, it has been discovered that three items had not been accounted for.

(i)   On 1 April 20X1, the company issued 100,000 new ordinary shares at a price of 80 cents per share.
(ii)   Closing inventory had been over stated by $10,000.
(iii) The directors wished to make a transfer to the general reserve of $5,000.

8   The amended balance on retained earnings at 31 March 20X2 was $ _____

9   Fill in the figure below.

$
Share capital   _____

10   Fill in the figures below.

Share premium   _____
General reserve   _____

19 Manufacturing accounts

1   The following information is for the year ended 31 October 20X0.

	$
Purchases of raw materials	56,000
Returns inwards	4,000
Increase in inventory of raw materials	1,700
Direct wages	21,000
Carriage inwards	2,500
Production overheads	14,000
Decrease in work-in-progress	5,000

The value of factory cost of goods completed is _____

2   The prime cost of goods manufactured is the total of:

A   Raw materials consumed
B   Raw materials consumed and direct wages
C   Raw materials consumed, direct wages and direct expenses
D   Raw materials consumed, direct wages, direct expenses and production overheads

3   The following information relates to a company at its year end.

	$
Inventory at beginning of year:	
Raw materials	10,000
Work-in-progress	2,000
Finished goods	34,000
Inventory at end of year:	
Raw materials	11,000
Work-in-progress	4,000
Finished goods	30,000
Purchases of raw materials	50,000
Direct wages	40,000
Royalties on goods sold	3,000
Production overheads	60,000
Distribution costs	55,000
Administration expenses	70,000
Sales	300,000

The cost of goods manufactured during the year is:

A $147,000
B $151,000
C $153,000
D $154,000

4   If work-in-progress (WIP) decreases during the period, then:

A   Prime cost will decrease
B   Prime cost will increase
C   The factory cost of goods completed will decrease
D   The factory cost of goods completed will increase

5   The prime cost of goods manufactured is the total of:

A   All factory costs before adjusting for work-in-progress
B   All factory costs of goods completed
C   All materials and labour
D   Direct factory costs

6   In manufacturing accounts, is depreciation on the factory part of the prime cost or an indirect cost?

A   Prime cost
B   Indirect cost

7   An increase in the figure for work-in-progress will:

A   Increase the prime cost
B   Decrease the prime cost
C   Increase the cost of goods sold
D   Decrease the factory cost of goods completed

8   At the start of the year, a manufacturing company had inventories of raw materials of $18,000 and inventories of finished goods of $34,000. There was no work in progress.

During the year, the following expenses were incurred:

	$
Raw materials purchased	163,000
Manufacturing expenses incurred	115,000

During the year, sales of $365,000 were made. The inventories of raw materials at the year end were valued at $21,000 and the inventories of finished goods were valued at $38,000. There was no work in progress.

The gross profit for the year is $ _____ .

9   The production cost of finished goods is?

A   Prime cost plus production overheads plus opening WIP less closing WIP

B   Prime cost plus production overheads

C   Prime cost plus opening WIP less closing WIP

D   Prime cost plus opening inventory of materials less closing inventory of materials plus production overheads

10 You are given the following information for the year ended 31 October 20X7:

	$
Purchases of raw materials	112,000
Returns inwards	8,000
Decrease in inventories of raw materials	8,000
Direct wages	42,000
Carriage outwards	4,000
Carriage inwards	3,000
Production overheads	27,000
Increase in work-in-progress	10,000

The value of factory cost of goods completed is:

A $174,000
B $182,000
C $183,000
D $202,000

11 The following information relates to NV Co for the year ended 31 July 20X3.

	$'000
Direct materials	160
Direct labour	200
Prime cost	360
Carriage outwards	880
Depreciation of delivery vehicles	30
Factory indirect overheads	450
Increase in work-in-progress inventory	75
Decrease in inventory of finished goods	55

What should be the factory cost of goods completed for the year ended 31 July 20X3?

12   Your firm has the following manufacturing figures.

	$
Prime cost	56,000
Factory overheads	4,500
Opening work-in-progress	6,200
Factory cost of goods completed	57,000

Closing work-in-progress is:

A $700
B $2,700
C $9,700
D $11,700

The following data relates to questions 13 to 15.

Balances at 31 December 20X4

	$
Non-current assets (cost $60,000)	39,000
Inventories	
Raw materials	25,000
Work in progress, valued at prime cost	5,800
Finished goods	51,000

The following relevant transactions occurred during 20X5.

	$
Invoiced purchases of raw materials, less returns	80,000
Discounts received	1,700
Factory wages paid	34,000
Indirect manufacturing expenses paid	61,900

Balances at 31 December 20X5

	$
Non-current assets (cost $90,000)	60,000
Inventories	
Raw materials	24,000
Work in progress	5,000
Finished goods	52,000

13   The prime cost of production for the year ended 31 December 20X5 was $ _____ .

---

14   The total depreciation charge for the year ended 31 December 20X5 was $ _____ .

---

15   During the year ended 31 December 20X6, the following expenditure was incurred:

	$
Prime cost	720,000
Factory overheads	72,000
The closing work in progress was	$350,000

The factory cost of goods completed during the year was $ _____ .

20 Statements of cash flows

1 In a statement of cash flows, interest paid appears under which heading?

    A   Cash flows from operating activities
    B   Investing activities
    C   Financing activities
    D   Cash and cash equivalents

2 APM provides the following note to non-current assets in its statement of financial position.

Plant and machinery

	Cost	Depreciation	Carrying value
	$'000	$'000	$'000
Opening balance	25	12	13
Additions/charge	15	4	11
Disposals	(10)	(8)	(2)
Closing balance	30	8	22

The additional machinery was purchased for cash. A machine was sold at a profit of $2,000.

What is the net cash outflow for plant and machinery?

    A $9,000
    B $11,000
    C $13,000
    D $15,000

3 The following information relates to CFS:

	$'000
Machinery	
Cost at 1 January 20X2	80
Additions	20
Disposal	(10)
Cost at 31 December 20X2	90
Accumulated depreciation at 1 January 20X2	15
Depreciation charge	8
Disposal	(6)
Accumulated depreciation at 31 December 20X2	17

The proceeds on disposal of the machine were $1,000.

CFS is preparing the statement of cash flows for the year ended 31 December 20X2. In relation to the items above, what should the net adjustment be to operating profit in order to determine the net cash flow from operating activities?

    A   Deduct $11,000
    B   Add back $3,000
    C   Add back $5,000
    D   Add back $11,000

4   When comparing two statements of financial position, you notice that:

   (i)   Last year, the company had included in current assets investments of $10,000. This year, there are no investments in current assets.

   (ii) Last year, the company had an overdraft of $8,000. This year, the overdraft is $4,000.

   What is the impact on the cash balance year on year?

   A   Increase $4,000
   B   Decrease $4,000
   C   Increase $6,000
   D   Decrease $6,000

---

5   The following information was extracted from the statements of financial position of Z at 31 December 20X2 and at 31 December 20X1:

	20X2	20X1
	$'000	$'000
Inventory	100	140
Receivables	150	130
Trade payables	125	115
Other payables	60	75

   What figure should appear as part of the statement of cash flows for the year ended 31 December 20X2?

   $ [   ]   [   ]
                    Inflow/outflow

---

6   A business has the following payments and receipts during its accounting period.

   •   Issue of shares $500,000
   •   Loan repaid $250,000
   •   Share premium received $150,000
   •   Proceeds of a rights issue $350,000
   •   Interest paid $120,000

   What is the financing cash flow?

   A $750,000
   B $630,000
   C $1,000,000
   D $600,000

---

7   A company has the following non-current asset transactions.

   •   Purchases of non-current assets costing $1,500,000
   •   Profit on sales of assets $50,000 (carrying amount $250,000)
   •   Depreciation charged $125,000.

   What is the investing cash flow?

   A $1,200,000 outflow
   B $1,075,000 inflow
   C $1,200,000 inflow
   D $1,075,000 outflow

8   In a statement of cash flows, purchase of non-current assets appears under which heading?

    A   Cash flows from operating activities
    B   Investing activities
    C   Financing activities
    D   Cash and cash equivalents

9   In a statement of cash flows, the issue of shares appears under which heading?

    A   Cash flows from operating activities
    B   Investing activities
    C   Financing activities
    D   Cash and cash equivalents

10 The following information is an extract from the statements of financial position of DCF.

	31 August 20X3 $'000	31 August 20X2 $'000
Inventory	20	14
Trade receivables	16	18
Bank	12	10
	48	42
Trade payables	(14)	(17)
	34	25

    DCF is preparing the statement of cash flows for the year end 31 August 20X3. In relation to the items above, what should be the net adjustment to operating profit in order to determine the net cash flow from operating activities?

    A   Deduct $1,000
    B   Deduct $2,000
    C   Deduct $7,000
    D   Add back $1,000

11 Which of the following items could appear in a company's statement of cash flows?

    1   Surplus on revaluation of non-current assets
    2   Proceeds of issue of shares
    3   Proposed dividend
    4   Irrecoverable debts written off
    5   Dividends received

    A   1, 2 and 5 only
    B   2, 3, 4, 5 only
    C   2 and 5 only
    D   3 and 4 only

12   Part of the process of preparing a company's statement of cash flows is the calculation of cash inflow from operating activities.

Which of the following statements about that calculation (using the indirect method) are correct?

1   Loss on sale of operating non-current assets should be deducted from net profit before taxation.
2   Increase in inventory should be deducted from operating profits.
3   Increase in payables should be added to operating profits.
4   Depreciation charges should be added to net profit before taxation.

A   1, 2 and 3
B   1, 2 and 4
C   1, 3 and 4
D   2, 3 and 4

The following information is relevant to questions 13 to 15.

Extracts from the draft financial statements for a company GH are as follows:

Statement of financial position extract as at 31 December 20X2

	31.12.X2 $	31.12.X1 $
Non-current assets		
Property, plant and equipment	240,000	210,000
Current assets		
Inventory	168,000	159,000
Receivables	132,000	154,000
Cash	140,000	124,000
Current liabilities		
Trade payables	41,000	33,000
Tax liability	25,000	21,000

Statement of profit or loss extract as at 31 December 20X2

	31.12.X2 $
Operating profit	142,000
Finance cost	(18,000)
Profit before tax	124,000
Tax	(22,000)
Net profit	102,000

Included within the statement of profit or loss is depreciation $18,900.

13   How much was spent by GH on non-current asset additions during the year?

$_____

---

14   How much tax was paid to the tax authorities during the year?

$_____

---

15   What is the net increase/(decrease) in cash and cash equivalents in the year?

$_____

---

21 Interpreting company accounts

1   During the year ended 31 October 20X7, your organisation made a gross profit of $60,000, which represented a mark-up of 50%. Opening inventory was $12,000 and closing inventory was $18,000.

The rate of inventory turnover was:

A   4 times
B   6.7 times
C   7.3 times
D   8 times

2   A business has the following trading account for the year ending 31 May 20X8:

	$	$
Revenue		45,000
Opening inventory	4,000	
Purchases	26,500	
	30,500	
Less closing inventory	6,000	
		24,500
Gross profit		20,500

Its rate of inventory turnover for the year is:

A   4.9 times
B   5.3 times
C   7.5 times
D   9 times

3   A company's gearing ratio would rise if:

A   The percentage decrease in non-current loans is **less** than the percentage decrease in shareholders' funds

B   The percentage decrease in non-current loans is **more** than the percentage decrease in shareholders' funds

C   Interest rates rose

D   Equity shares were issued

4   A company has the following details extracted from its statement of financial position:

	$'000
Inventories	1,900
Receivables	1,000
Bank overdraft	100
Payables	1,000

Its liquidity position could be said to be:

A   Very well-controlled because its current assets far outweigh its current liabilities
B   Poorly controlled because its quick assets are less than its current liabilities
C   Poorly controlled because its current ratio is significantly higher than the industry norm of 1.8
D   Poorly controlled because it has a bank overdraft

The gross profit mark-up is 40% where:

A   Sales are $120,000 and gross profit is $48,000
B   Sales are $120,000 and cost of sales is $72,000
C   Sales are $100,800 and cost of sales is $72,000
D   Sales are $100,800 and cost of sales is $60,480

---

6   From the following information regarding the year to 31 August 20X6, what is the payables' payment period?

	$
Sales	43,000
Cost of sales	32,500
Opening inventory	6,000
Closing inventory	3,800
Payables at 31 August 20X6	4,750

A   40 days
B   50 days
C   53 days
D   57 days

---

7   The draft statement of financial position of B at 31 March 20X8 is set out below.

		$ '000s	$'000s
Non-current assets			450
Current assets:	Inventory	65	
	Receivables	110	
	Prepayments	30	
		205	
Current liabilities	Payables	30	
	Bank overdraft (Note)	50	
		80	
			125
			575
Long-term liability:	Loan		(75)
			500
Ordinary share capital			400
Statement of profit or loss			100
			500

Note. The bank overdraft first occurred on 30 September 20X7.

What is the gearing of the company?

A   13%
B   16%
C   20%
D   24%

8   What is the formula for calculating the current ratio?

A $\dfrac{\text{Cost of sales}}{\text{Inventories}}$

B $\dfrac{\text{Trade payables}}{\text{Cost of sales}} \times 365 \text{ days}$

C $\dfrac{\text{Current assets}}{\text{Current liabilities}}$

D $\dfrac{\text{Profit for the year}}{\text{Revenue}} \times 100$

9   Working capital is?

A   Non-current assets + net current assets
B   Current assets – current liabilities
C   Total assets – total liabilities
D   Liquid current assets – current liabilities

10   A firm buys materials on 2 months' credit, and they spend 2 months in inventory and 0.5 months in production. Finished goods are normally retained for 3 months before sale and on average, receivables take 3 months to pay.

Calculate the time taken for cash to cycle through the business.

A   6.5 months
B   8.5 months
C   3.5 months
D   2.5 months

11   Arrange the following current assets in order of increasing liquidity (least to most liquid).

(i)   Inventory
(ii)   Cash
(iii) Receivables
(iv)   Prepayments

A   (ii), (iv), (iii), (i)
B   (i), (ii), (iii), (iv)
C   (i), (iii), (iv), (ii)
D   (iv), (ii), (iii), (i)

12   A business operates on a gross profit margin of $33\frac{1}{3}\%$. Gross profit on a sale was $800, and expenses were $680. The net profit percentage is:

A   3.75%
B   5%
C   11.25%
D   22.67%

Use these summarised accounts to answer Questions 13 to 15

SUMMARISED STATEMENT OF FINANCIAL POSITION AT 31 DECEMBER 20X4

		$'000	$'000
Non-current assets			4,700
Current assets:	Inventory	1,200	
	Receivables	1,700	
	Cash	300	
			3,200
			7,900

	$'000
Capital and reserves	
Ordinary $1 share capital	2,000
Preference share capital	400
Retained profits	1,000
	3,400
10% loan stock	3,000
Current liabilities	
Payables	1,500
	7,900

SUMMARISED STATEMENT OF PROFIT OR LOSS AT 31 DECEMBER 20X4

	$'000
Revenue	12,000
Cost of sales	7,000
Gross profit	5,000
Operating expenses	(2,500)
Operating profit	2,500
Debenture interest	(300)
Profit before taxation	2,200
Taxation	(700)
	1,500
Preference dividend	20

13   Non-current asset turnover is:

    A   0.781 times
    B   1.875 times
    C   2.553 times
    D   3.529 times

14   The gross profit margin is:

	Gross
A	21%
B	71%
C	18%
D	42%

15 Inventory days and receivables days are:

	Inventory days	Receivables days
A	36	52
B	36	88
C	63	52
D	63	88

22 The Framework

1   Listed below are some comments on accounting concepts.

1   Financial statements always treat the business as a separate entity.

2   Materiality means that only items having a physical existence may be recognised as assets.

3   Provisions are estimates and therefore can be altered to make the financial results of a business more attractive to investors.

Which, if any, of these comments is correct, according to the IASB's *Conceptual Framework for Financial Reporting*?

A   1 only
B   2 only
C   3 only
D   None of them

2   Sales revenue should be recognised when goods and services have been supplied; costs are incurred when goods and services have been received.

Which accounting concept governs the above?

A   The consistency concept
B   The materiality concept
C   The accruals concept
D   The duality concept

3   Which accounting concept states that omitting or misstating this information could influence users of the financial statements?

A   The consistency concept
B   The accruals concept
C   The materiality concept
D   The going concern concept

4   The IASB's *Conceptual Framework for Financial Reporting* gives four enhancing qualitative characteristics. What are these four characteristics?

A   Consistency, understandability, faithful representation, substance over form
B   Accruals basis, going concern concept, consistency, true and fair view
C   Faithful representation, comparability, understandability, relevance
D   Comparability, timeliness, understandability, verifiability

5   Which of the following may appear as current liabilities in a company's statement of financial position?

1   A revaluation surplus
2   Loan due for repayment within one year
3   Income tax payable
4   Preferred dividends payable on redeemable preference shares

A   1, 2 and 3
B   1, 2 and 4
C   1, 3 and 4
D   2, 3 and 4

6   According to the IASB's *Conceptual Framework for Financial Reporting*, which TWO of the following are part of faithful representation?

1   It is neutral
2   It is relevant
3   It is presented fairly
4   It is free from material error

A   1 and 2
B   2 and 3
C   1 and 4
D   3 and 4

7   Which basic accounting concept is being followed when a charge is made for depreciation?

A   Accruals
B   Consistency
C   Going concern
D   Materiality

8   If, at the end of the financial year, a company makes a charge against the profits for stationery consumed but not yet invoiced, this adjustment is in accordance with the concept of:

A   Materiality
B   Accruals
C   Consistency
D   Separate entity

9   Which qualitative characteristic of financial information can be achieved through a combination of consistency and disclosure?

A   Comparability
B   Understandability
C   Verifiability
D   Relevance

10   CIMA's recent annual report mentions how they create value from the interaction between CIMA employees, students, members, employers, partners and industry bodies and society.

Which type of capital does the above relate to, as defined by the International Integrated Reporting Council (IIRC)?

A   Natural capital
B   Financial capital
C   Human capital
D   Social and relationship capital

---

11   The accounting concept to be considered when the owner of a business uses business funds to pay for his private household expenses, is the:

A   Separate entity concept
B   Fair presentation concept
C   Accruals concept
D   Going concern concept

---

12   Dee has given you a piece of paper with two statements about accounting concepts.

(a)   A business continues in existence for the foreseeable future.
(b)   Revenues and expenses should be recognised in the period in which they are earned or incurred.

Name the two accounting concepts described above.

1   _____

2   _____

The following information is relevant to questions 13 to 15

You have recently been appointed as assistant accountant of PQR Co. You have assisted in preparing a forecast set of final accounts for the company whose year end is 31 December 20X7. The forecast shows that the company is expected to make a loss during the year to 31 December 20X7. This would be the first time that the company has made a loss since it was incorporated 20 years ago.

The managing director is concerned that the company's shareholders would be unhappy to hear that the company had made a loss. He is determined to avoid making a loss if at all possible.

He has made a number of suggestions in order to rectify the situation.

13   State whether you agree with the following suggestion made by the managing director:

'Make no further provision for obsolete inventory and consider crediting the statement of comprehensive income with the provision made in previous years.'

YES/NO

---

14   State whether you agree with the following suggestion made by the managing director:

'Do not allow for depreciation for the year to 31 December 20X7.'

YES/NO

15   State whether you agree with the following suggestion made by the managing director.

'Capitalise all research expenditure'.

YES/NO

23 The regulatory system

1   What is the role of the International Financial Reporting Standards (IFRS) Interpretations Committee?

    A   Oversee the standard setting and regulatory process
    B   Formulate international financial reporting standards
    C   Review defective accounts
    D   Issues guidance on how to apply IFRS

2   What is the role of the International Financial Reporting Standards (IFRS)?

    A   To ensure financial statements are correct
    B   To give accountancy students material to study
    C   To provide instructions as to how items should be shown in a set of financial statements
    D   To provide guidance on how to apply IFRS

3   Who raises finance to support the regulatory system?

    A   IFRS Foundation
    B   IFRS Advisory Council
    C   International Accounting Standards Board
    D   IFRS Interpretations Committee

4   Which body liaises with national accounting standard setters to achieve convergence?

    A   IFRS Foundation
    B   IFRS Advisory Council
    C   International Accounting Standards Board
    D   IFRS Interpretations Committee

5   Identify one of the roles of the International Accounting Standards Board.

    A   Oversee the standard setting and regulatory process
    B   Formulate international financial reporting standards
    C   Raise finance for the regulatory process
    D   Provide guidance on the international financial reporting standards

6   Who issues International Financial Reporting Standards?

    A   The IFRS Advisory Committee
    B   The stock exchange
    C   The International Accounting Standards Board
    D   The government

7   What is the role of the IASB?

    A   Oversee the standard setting and regulatory process
    B   Formulate international financial reporting standards
    C   Review defective accounts
    D   Control the accountancy profession

8   Which of the following provides advice to the International Accounting Standards Board (IASB) as well as informing the IASB of the implications of proposed standards for users and preparers of financial statements?

    A   The IFRS Advisory Council
    B   The IFRS Interpretations Committee
    C   The IFRS Foundation
    D   The Trustees

9   Who does the IFRS Interpretations Committee report to?

    A   International Accounting Standards Committee Foundation
    B   Standards Advisory Council
    C   International Accounting Standards Board
    D   The Trustees

10   The IFRS Foundation appoints the members of which other bodies?

    A   IFRS Advisory Council

    B   International Accounting Standards Board

    C   IFRS Interpretations Committee

    D   The IFRS Advisory Council, the International Accounting Standards Board and the IFRS Interpretations Committee

11   Which of the following statements is/are true?

    1   The IFRS Interpretations Committee is a forum for the IASB to consult with the outside world.

    2   The IFRS Foundation produces IFRSs. The IFRS Foundation is overseen by the IASB.

    3   One of the objectives of the IFRS Foundation is to bring about convergence of national accounting standards and IFRSs.

    A   1 and 3 only
    B   2 only
    C   2 and 3 only
    D   3 only

12   Fill in the blanks.

The IFRS _____ _____ issues _____ _____ which aid users' interpretation of IFRSs.

The following information is relevant for Questions 13 to 15

Denise has just started at your firm as an accounts assistant. You have asked her to prepare some notes on the regulatory framework of accounts. She has submitted this below, but there are a number of errors in her notes.

13   Regulations on the financial statements of all companies come from four main sources:

   (i)   Company Law
   (ii)   National GAAP/International Financial Reporting Standards
   (iii)   Taxation authorities
   (iv)   The Stock Exchange

   Which of Denise's statements about regulations on the financial statements of all companies is true?

   A   (i)
   B   (i) and (ii)
   C   (i), (ii) and (iii)
   D   (i), (ii), (iii), and (iv)

14   The following are objectives of the IFRS Foundation:

   (i)   Through the IASB, develop a single set of globally accepted International Financial Reporting Standards (IFRSs)

   (ii)   Promote the use and rigorous application of International Financial Reporting Standards (IFRSs)

   (iii)   Ensure International Financial Reporting Standards (IFRSs) focus primarily on the needs of global, multi-national organisations

   (iv)   Bring about the convergence of national accounting standards and IFRSs

   Which of Denise's statements about the objectives of the IFRS Foundation is NOT correct?

   A   (i)
   B   (ii)
   C   (iii)
   D   (iv)

15   International Financial Reporting Standards (IFRSs) should be used:

   (i)   To provide examples of best financial reporting practice for national bodies who develop their own requirements

   (ii)   To ensure high ethical standards are maintained by financial reporting professionals internationally

   (iii)   To facilitate the enforcement of a single set of global financial reporting standards

   (iv)   To prevent national bodies from developing their own financial reporting standards

   Which of Denise's statements about how IFRSs are used is true?

   A   (i)
   B   (i) and (ii)
   C   (i), (ii) and (iii)
   D   (i), (ii), (iii), and (iv)

Answers

1 The nature and objective of accounting

1
- ☐ Stock market analysts
- ☑ Company employees
- ☑ The company's bank
- ☐ Institutional shareholders
- ☑ Suppliers

The employees, the bank and the suppliers will be interested.

Neither stock market analysts nor institutional shareholders (large owners of company shares eg pension funds) would be interested in investing in a small private company.

2
- ☑ To show the results of management's stewardship of the resources entrusted to it

- ☐ To provide a basis for valuing the entity

- ☑ To provide information about the financial position, financial performance and cash flows of an entity that is useful to a wide range of users in making economic decisions

- ☐ To facilitate comparison of financial performance between entities operating in different industries

- ☐ To assist management and those charged with governance in making timely economic decisions about deployment of the entity's resources

International Accounting Standard 1 (IAS 1) *Presentation of Financial Statements* explains the objective of financial statements. It states that the purpose of financial statements is to provide information about the financial position, financial performance and cash flows of an entity that is useful to a wide range of users in making economic decisions (C). In addition, it states that the financial statements also show the results of management's stewardship of the resources entrusted to it (A).

3   D   Generally Accepted Accounting Principles

4
- ☑ Establish levels of tax revenue
- ☐ Assess whether the business will continue in existence
- ☑ Produce national statistics
- ☐ Assess the owner's stewardship
- ☐ Take decisions about their investment

Both tax and national statistics will apply to the needs of government and its agencies. Whether the business will continue as a going concern (B) is an issue for the sole trader, its suppliers, customers and employees. The sole trader is interested in their own stewardship (D) of the business's resources; this is really only an issue for company owners, as is (E).

5   B   By law, it is the board of directors that is responsible for preparing financial statements.

6   1   Employees
     2   The government

7   C   There are too many activities for a manager to keep track of by himself and so he needs accounts which summarise transactions to monitor the business' performance.

8   The main distinction between financial accounting and management accounting is that financial accounting provides **historical** information to people **outside** the organisation, whereas management accounting provides **forward-looking** information to **management** on which they can base **decisions**.

9   B   Correct.

Borrowings are liabilities of a business, not capital. Capital will always equal net assets employed at a point in time. Loan capital could be provided, so this definition is not precise.

10   B   A sole trader does not have any shareholders. The accounts are unlikely to be of interest to a financial analyst, they are more usually interested in the accounts of public companies.

11   B   (2) is the IASB's Conceptual framework description of the purpose of financial statements. (1) is false – although a shareholder needs to know about a company's future prospects, they also need to know that the current position of the company is secure. Similarly, a supplier needs to know the future prospects of a company to ensure that he will be paid.

12   D   A relates to the statement of profit or loss, B and C suggest that the statement of financial position represents a valuation which is incorrect, while D is correct in that it is the definition of a statement of financial position's purpose.

13

☑	Prepares accounts for internal use
☐	Prepares accounts for external use
☑	Prepares budgets
☑	Compares actual performance with budget
☑	Costs products
☐	Prepares accounts under IFRS
☐	Prepares the statement of financial position and statement of profit of loss
☐	Prepares historic accounts

The management accountant prepares information for use by the company on an internal level. Therefore, their main roles are preparing budgets and comparing actual performance against these budgets. Management accountants also look at product costings and profit margins which are required in the preparation of budgets.

14

☐	Prepares accounts for internal use
☑	Prepares accounts for external use
☐	Prepares budgets
☐	Compares actual performance with budget
☐	Costs products
☑	Prepares accounts under IFRS
☑	Prepares the statement of financial position and statement of profit of loss
☑	Prepares historic accounts

The financial accountant will prepare accounts for external use using historical data. External accounts must be prepared in line with local or internal accounting standards (GAAP, IFRS). As part of that external reporting, a company is required to prepare a statement of profit or loss and a statement of financial position.

15   The correct answer is: $550

Under the accruals basis of accounting, income and expenditure are included in the statement of profit or loss in the period in which they are incurred, not received or paid. Therefore:

Sales in April:

	$
	2,000
	3,000
Total	5,000

Purchases in April:

	$
	950
	3,500
Total	4,450

Sales less purchases = 5,000 – 4,450 = 550

The receipts and payments information is irrelevant to calculating the profit.

---

2 An introduction to final accounts

1   A   Assets increase, as cash on receipt of the loan funds; and liabilities will increase, as the loan is a liability.

2   B   Assets will increase, as there is an increase in cash of $500 and a decrease in inventory of only $300; and capital will increase due to the profit of $200.

3   C   The car increases assets but it is treated as capital introduced rather than as a liability of the business to its proprietor.

4   B   Closing capital/net assets = opening capital + profit + additional capital - drawings

= $95,100 = opening capital + $35,400 + $10,200 - $6,000 ($500 × 12)

$95,100 - $35,400 - $10,200 + $6,000 = $55,500

5   C   Assets – liabilities = opening capital + profits – drawings

Therefore, assets – liabilities – opening capital + drawings = profit

6   A $3,200 loss

Closing capital = opening capital + additional capital – drawings +/(–) profit/(loss)

$73,800 = $75,600 + $17,700 - $16,300 +/(–) profit/(loss)

$73,800 = $77,000 +/(–) profit/(loss)

$73,800 = $77,000 - $3,200 loss

7   C   The accounting equation:

Assets = Opening capital + profit − drawings + liabilities

can be rewritten as:

Assets − liabilities − opening capital + drawings = profit.

8   D   Petrol being paid in petty cash means assets decrease and drawings increase, which decreases capital. Option A is a switch between assets, while options B and C increase assets and increase liabilities.

9   C   Assets − liabilities = opening capital + profits − drawings

Therefore, assets − liabilities − opening capital + drawings = profit

10   D $180,000

Closing net assets = opening net assets + additional capital − drawings + profit

$180,000 = $101,700 + $8,000 - $2,200 + $72,500

11   A   The overdraft liability will decrease, and receivables will decrease by an equal amount.

12   A   Assets will increase as the sole trader has acquired inventory, and liabilities will increase as the goods were purchased on credit.

13   C   (i) (iii) and (iv)

These items are capital expenditure as they increase the earning capacity of the business.

Repairing a broken window is expenditure incurred for the purpose of maintaining a non-current asset (a building), which is one of the definitions of revenue expenditure.

Purchase of ink for printers is expenditure incurred for the purpose of trade, which is one of the definitions of revenue expenditure.

14   B   Capital expenditure is expenditure which results in the acquisition of non-current assets, or an improvement in their earning capacity.

'Capital' in the statement of financial position refers to the amount of funds invested in a business and should not be confused with capital expenditure.

15   B   Since the items have not been paid for, this gives rise to a trade payable − a supplier who the business owes money to.

3 Sources, records and the books of prime entry

1   B   The exact amount of petty cash expenditure is reimbursed at intervals to maintain a fixed float.

2   B   A, C and D are all ledgers to which transactions are posted from the books of original entry. The journal (B) is the book of original entry that is used for unusual transactions; and to correct errors and omissions.

3

☐	Sales order
☑	Purchase order
☐	Remittance advice
☑	Goods received note
☐	Credit note

4   C   Discounts allowed, like discounts received, are recorded in the cash book as the book of original entry.

5   A   VAT on credit sales is recorded in the sales day book (A). VAT on cash sales and on credit purchases would be recorded in the cash book (C); and purchases day book, respectively.

6   A   A debit note is sent to a supplier with a return of goods. A debit note is, in effect, a request for a credit note.

7   B   The journal, cash book and sales day book are books of prime entry.

8   B   Credit notes received from suppliers are recorded in the purchase returns day book.

9   B   Discounts allowed are recorded in the cash book. Credit notes received are to do with returned purchases (not sales). Trade discounts are not recorded, as they are deducted on the sales invoices and only the net sale is recorded.

10   D   Credit notes for returns appear in the purchase returns day book (returns outwards).

11   C   The cash receipts book is summarised and posted to the general ledger. The other three are posted to the receivables/payables control accounts.

12   C   Direct debits are recorded in the cash payments book.

13   C   The purchases day book is the book of prime entry which is used to record invoices from suppliers for credit purchases only.

              The purchase of stationary is by petty cash and is therefore recorded in the petty cash book and not the purchases day book.

              Payment to supplier Z Computers is recorded in the cash payments book.

14   B   The sales day book is used to record invoices to customers for credit sales only.

              The cash sale is not a credit sale. It is recorded in the cash book, which records all bank transactions.

              The return of goods from the customer, although linked to a credit sale, is recorded in a separate day book, the sales returns day book.

15   A   Both (i) cash sale of goods to Customers A Davis $200 and (iv) Payment to supplier Z Computers $900 would be recorded in the cash book.

              Petty cash transactions are recorded in a separate petty cash book.

4 Ledger accounting and double entry

1   C   The asset account and expense account would normally be debit balances.

2   A   Cash and credit sales are credit entries, whilst irrecoverable debts do not appear in the sales account.

3

✓	Incurring an expense results in a debit to the expense account
✓	Decrease in a liability results in a debit to the liability account
	Increase in an asset results in a credit to the asset account
	Decrease in an asset results in a debit to the asset account
✓	Increase in a liability results in a credit to the liability account

Debit entries increase asset (or reduce liabilities) in the statement of financial position and increase expenses (or reduce income) in the statement of profit or loss.

Credit entries increase liabilities (or reduce assets) in the statement of financial position and increase income (or reduce expenses) in the statement of profit or loss.

4   C

TRADE PAYABLES ACCOUNT

	$		$
Cash at bank	100,750	Balance b/d	250,225
Balance c/d	474,485	Purchases	325,010
	575,235		575,235
		Balance b/d	474,485

5   D   Remember that only credit purchases are listed in the purchases daybook.

6   D   A record of amounts owed to/from individual suppliers and customers is the trade payables/receivables ledgers. An initial record of internally generated transactions is the journal, and a list of assets and liabilities is the statement of financial position.

7   B   Increase in an asset, as it would result in a debit. All others are incorrect. They would all result in a credit.

8   C   Credit entries increase liabilities.

Credit entries decrease assets.

Debit entries increase expenses.

9   C   DR Purchases $400
            DR Trade Payables $250
               CR Cash and bank $650

A payment is a credit to the cash account. The payment to J Bloggs is a cash purchase and so the double entry is Dr Purchases, Cr Cash. Remember that the purchase from J Doe has already been recorded as Dr Purchases, Cr Trade Payables, so the payment of cash to clear the invoice should now be recorded as Dr Trade Payables, Cr Cash.

10	C	You are recording the transaction in Steel Co's books – Steel Co is the seller, so the double entry is DR receivables $250, CR sales $250.

11	A	DR Trade receivables	$150	
		DR Sales Returns	$300	
		CR Revenue		$150
		CR Cash and bank		$300

The double entry for the sale of goods on credit is DR Trade receivables, CR Revenue $150. The return of goods previously sold for cash is DR Sales Returns, CR Cash and bank $300.

12	D	Correct.
	A	This ledger is used to record impersonal accounts.
	B	Customers' accounts are kept in the sales ledger.
	C	This is simply a record of purchase invoices received.

13		DEBIT: CASH AND BANK $50; CREDIT: SALES $50
14		DEBIT: NON-CURRENT ASSETS $1,000; CREDIT: CASH AND BANK $1,000
15		DEBIT: RECEIVABLES $450; CREDIT: REVENUE $450

5 From trial balance to final accounts

1	A	The closing inventory may be calculated after taking into account cost of sales and purchases.
2	B	The omitted balance is an asset account and thus a debit. So in the trial balance the total of **credit** balances will exceed the total of debit balances by $2,000.
3	A	Current assets are inventory ($4,500) and trade receivables ($5,000)
4	B	This is an error of original entry.
5	A	Items 2, 3 and 4 preserve double entry and so would not show up in a trial balance.
6	B	The cash book was credited with $210 reimbursement of petty cash. However, the nominal ledger was posted with only $200 of expenditure (debits). Therefore, the credits are $10 higher than the debits.
7	D	Debits will exceed credits by $2 \times \$48 = \$96$
8	D	Errors of principle, such as recording a capital expenditure transaction as revenue expenditure, would not be revealed by a trial balance because it would not create an inequality between total debits and total credits. Transposition errors are errors where figures (digits) are written in the wrong order in either a credit or a debit entry. This would create an imbalance between credits and debts, and so the error would be indicated by extracting a trial balance.

BPP
LEARNING MEDIA

9	A	The debits are as follows	

	$
Opening inventory	9,649
Purchases	124,958
Expenses	34,835
Non-current assets	63,960
Receivables	31,746
Cash at bank	1,783
	266,931

10 C A transaction has been posted to the wrong account, but not the wrong class of account.

11 B In option 2, receivables and drawings are debits, but discount received is a credit. In option 4, capital and trade payables are credits, but operating expenses are debits.

12 D This is an example of a failure of the basic rules of double entry, so the trial balance will not agree.

  A This is an error of omission, the financial records will be incomplete but the integrity of the double entry process is not impaired.

  B This is an error of principle, confusion between capital and revenue expenditure has occurred.

  C This is a reversal error, the trial balance will agree because debits = credits, however the accounts are incorrect.

13	D	DR	Purchases	$100	
		CR	Bank		$100

14	C	DR	Trade receivables	$500	
		CR	Revenue		$500

15

Cash and bank (3,255 – 100)	3,155	
Capital		15,500
Rent	2,225	
Trade payables		14,450
Purchases (13,150 + 100)	13,250	
Revenue (14,600 + 500)		15,100
Other payables		1,620
Trade receivables (12,000 + 500)	12,500	
Other expenses	13,520	
Vehicles	2,020	
Total	46,670	46,670

6 Tangible non-current assets

1 B False

While the non-current asset register should agree with the nominal ledger, this will not always be the case. There may be items that have been posted to the register or the nominal ledger but not both, resulting in differences between the balances. Similarly, there may be errors in the register or in the nominal ledger which also means that they will not agree until the errors are corrected.

2 A Annual depreciation = $\dfrac{\$120,000 - 4,000}{4\ \text{years}}$

= $29,000

Depreciation charge 1 Oct – 31 Dec = $29,000 × 3/12 = $7,250

3 B This receipt will eliminate the insurance receivable and reduce the loss on disposal by $500.

4 B

		Carrying value
Purchase price		80,000
20X2	75%	60,000
20X3	75%	45,000
20X4	75%	33,750
20X5	75%	25,312

5 D

	$	$
Original cost	24,000	
Residual value	(2,000)	
	22,000	
Annual depreciation (22,000 / 5)		4,400
31 December 20X1		
Original cost	24,000	
2 years depreciation	(8,800)	
	15,200	
Annual depreciation (15,200 / 2)		7,600

6 C

7 C

	$
Profit	8,000
Add back depreciation	12,000
Net cash inflow	20,000
Purchase of non-current assets for cash	(25,000)
Decrease in cash	5,000

8 Loss on disposal = $87

	$
9,000 × 0.7 × 0.7 × 0.7 =	3,087 (carrying value
Proceeds of sale	(3,000)
Loss on disposal	87

As this is the reducing balance method, the residual value is included in the 30% rate.

9   The accounting concept which dictates that non-current assets should be valued at cost, less accumulated depreciation, rather than their enforced saleable value.

10   Loss on disposal = $360

	$
Carrying amount ($5,000 × 0.8 × 0.8 × 0.8)	2,560
Proceeds	(2,200)
Loss on disposal	360

Remember this is the reducing balance method, the residual value is included in the 20% rate.

11   By charging depreciation in the accounts, a business aims to ensure that the cost of non-current assets is **spread over the accounting periods** which benefit from their use.

12   Profit on sale = $1,500

	$
Carrying amount ($64,000 × 0.5 × 0.5 × 0.5 × 0.5)	4,000
Proceeds	(5,500)
Profit	1,500

As this is the reducing balance method, the residual value is included in the 50% rate.

13   D   Spread the net cost of the assets over their estimated useful life.

14   20X2 depreciation charge = $450

$$\text{Annual depreciation} = \frac{\text{Cost minus residual value}}{\text{Estimated life}}$$

$$\text{Annual depreciation charge} = \frac{\$1,800 - \$0}{4 \text{ years}}$$

20X2 depreciation = $450

15   20X2 depreciation charge = $432

	$	
Cost at 1.1.20X1	1,800	
Depreciation 20X1	1,080	60% × $1,800
Book value 1.1.20X2	720	
Depreciation 20X2	432	60% × $720
Book value 1.1.20X3	288	

7 Intangible non-current assets

1   A   Research expenditure is never capitalised.

2   D   Research expenditure is always expensed in the period of incurring the cost. It is not capitalised.

3   A   Research expenditure is never capitalised. Development expenditure is capitalised if it meets certain conditions, as per IAS 38.

Intangible assets with a finite life are amortised over their useful life. If the life of the asset is indefinite, then it is not amortised.

4	B	The patent should be amortised over its useful life of 10 years. Therefore the balance at 30 November 20X5 is $25,000 − ($25,000 × 2/10) = $20,000
5	B	The amortisation charge is $15,000 / 3 years = $5,000 per annum. The double entry to record the amortisation is DR expenses, CR accumulated amortisation.
6	C	An investment is not classified as an intangible non-current asset.
7	B	There is no requirement that development expenditure should be amortised over a period not exceeding five years.
8	C	Development expenditure must be capitalised if the criteria are met.
		There is no time scale given by IAS 38 for amortisation.
9	C	Development costs are amortised over the useful life of the project. This is not confined to a period of five years.
10	A	3 only.
		Option 1 is incorrect as there is no time scale given by IAS 38 for amortisation.
		Option 2 is incorrect as development expenditure must be capitalised if the criteria are met.
		Option 4 is incorrect as amortisation of capitalised development expenditures does not appear as an item in the statement of changes in equity.
11	B	A factory is a tangible asset as it has physical form. The others are intangible assets.
12	D	A patent has no physical substance and provides future economic benefits; it is therefore an intangible non-current asset.
		Computer hardware, machinery and a building extension are tangible non-current assets which provide economic benefits.
13	A	Amortisation is an application of the matching concept and allocates the cost of the intangible asset over its useful life (over the accounting periods expected to benefit from its use).
14	A	Research expenditure $103,000 + amortisation of development costs $20,000.
15	A	Development costs b/f $180,000 + additions on project 910 $59,000 − amortisation $20,000.

8 Cost of goods sold and inventories

1	B	Correct, $58,000 + $256,000 − $17,000 − $63,000 = $234,000.
	A	Incorrect, returns and inventory changes must be allowed for.
	C	Incorrect, changes in inventory levels must be allowed for.
	D	Incorrect, you have transposed opening and closing inventories.
2	A	Correct, FIFO will produce the highest valuation of closing inventory of the three methods, giving the higher profit figure.
	B	Incorrect, under LIFO costing closing inventory will be valued at the earlier prices.
	C	Incorrect, LIFO is not permissible under IAS 2.
	D	Incorrect, average cost will be recalculated after every new delivery into inventory occurs.

	Quantity	Cost	Net realisable value (95% of sales price)	Valuation Per unit	Total
Beads	2,000	$1.50	$1.4535	$1.4535	2,907
Buttons	1,500	$1.25	$1.33	$1.25	1,875
Bows	2,000	$1.60	$1.425	$1.425	2,850
					7,632

3 B

4 A

	$
50 @ $190	9,500
500 @ $220	110,000
300 @ $230	69,000
	188,500

5 B

	$
Original inventory valuation	41,875
Cost of damaged items	(1,960)
NRV of damaged items (1,200 – 360)	840
	40,755

6 C Debit closing inventory (SOFP), credit closing inventory (cost of sales, SPL)

Closing inventory is an asset in the statement of financial position at the year end and a reduction in expenses in cost of sales in the statement of profit or loss.

7 B $303,000

	$
Opening inventory	30,000
Purchases	296,000
Carriage inwards	11,000
Less Closing inventory	(34,000)
	303,000

8 C Correct, the inventory would be included at the lower of cost or NRV – assuming it was saleable at a profit, the appropriate cost would be that relating to its finished goods state.

9 The accruals concept

10 1 FIFO (first in, first out)
2 Average cost

11 D Gross profit – expenses = net profit.

12 C IAS 2 *Inventories* prohibits the use of LIFO.

13 B FIFO will lead to higher reported profit because his cost of sales will be based on the earliest (and therefore cheapest) purchases.

14	C	$2,000				
		Date	Units	Unit cost	Cost of issues $	Balance in inventory $
		1 March	50	$40		2,000
		17 March	50	$50		2,500
		31 March	−50	$40	2,000	
			−10	$50	500	
		Closing value	40	$50		2,000

15	B	$1,800				
		Date	Units	Unit cost	Cost of issues $	Balance in inventory $
		1 March	50	$40		2,000
		17 March	50	$50		2,500
			100	$45*		4,500
		31 March	−60	$45	2,700	
		Closing value	40	$45		1,800

* 4,500/100

9 Irrecoverable debts and allowances for receivables

1 A

	$
Irrecoverable debts written off	14,600
Reduction in allowance	(2,000)
	12,600

2 B

	$
Allowance required 5% × (864,000 − 13,000)	42,550
Existing allowance	(48,000)
Reduction in allowance	(5,450)
Irrecoverable debts written off	13,000
Statement of profit or loss charge	7,550

Net trade receivables = $864,000 − 13,000 − 42,550

= $808,450

3 A The debt needs to be written off. The allowance previously made will be adjusted at the year end.

4 C An increase in the allowance for receivables will reduce profits and receivables. Gross profit will not be affected since allowances for receivables are dealt with in the net profit section.

5   D

	$	SPL charge $
Receivables allowance at 31.12.X1 (5% of $20,000)	1,000	
Receivables allowance at 1.1.X1	3,000	
Decrease in allowance		2,000
Irrecoverable debts written off		(1,000)
Debt recovered		800
Total credit to statement of profit or loss		1,800

6   D   A decrease in the allowance is written back to profit.

7   C

ALLOWANCE FOR RECEIVABLES

	$		$
		b/d	850
C/d	1,000		
		Expense	150
	1,000		1,000

ALLOWANCE FOR RECEIVABLES

	$		$
Allowance	150		
Receivables	500	SPL	650
	650		650

8   D

	$
Closing allowance required (400,000 − 38,000) × 10%	36,200
Opening allowance	50,000
Decrease in allowance	(13,800)
Irrecoverable debts written off	38,000
Statement of profit or loss charge	24,200

9   C $146,000 + ($218,000 − $83,000) = $281,000

10   B   Because the debt has been previously written off, there is no receivable for which to offset the cash, therefore the double entry is DR Cash and bank, CR Irrecoverable debts expense.

11   A   When a business first establishes an allowance for receivables, the full amount of the allowance should be debited to irrecoverable debts (statement of profit or loss) and credited to allowance for receivables (statement of financial position).

12   D

	$
Irrecoverable debt written off	28,500
Increase in allowance ((868,500 − 28,500) × 5% − 38,000)	4,000
	32,500

13   D   A credit entry in the receivables account.

14 B Because the debt has been previously written off, there is no receivable for which to offset the cash; therefore the double entry is DR Cash and bank, CR irrecoverable debts expense.

15 C The new balance on the receivables will be $1,170 (($78,600 − $600) × 1.5%) This is a reduction of $30 from the previous balance of $1,200, which will be credited to the statement of profit or loss.

10 Accruals (and prepayments)

1 C

	$
1 Jan – 30 June (12,000 × 6/12)	6,000
1 July – 31 Dec (13,200 × 6/12)	6,600
	12,600

2 C

Accrued: $560; charge to SPL $3,320

ELECTRICITY ACCOUNT

		$		$
			Balance b/fwd	300
20X0				
1 August	Paid bank	600		
1 November	Paid bank	720		
20X1				
1 February	Paid bank	900		
30 June	Paid bank	840		
30 June	Accrual c/d			
($840 × ⅔)*		560	Statement of profit or loss	3,320
		3,620		3,620

* the last bill is used as the basis for the accrual to the year-end.

3 A Dr rental income $4,000; Cr current liabilities $4,000

MN makes payments of $4,000 ($48,000 / 12) in advance on the 1st of each month. Therefore, $4,000 received on 1 July 20X4 relates to the year ended 31 July 20X5. For this reason, at the year ended 31 July 20X4, it is posted as a debit to rental income (decreasing revenue for the year) and as a credit to current liabilities in the statement of financial position (being prepaid income).

4 B

Gas charges for two months have to be accrued

	DR	CR
Gas expense	1,400	
Accruals		1,400

5   B

	$
February to March 20X2 (22,500 × 2/3)	15,000
April to June	22,500
July to September	22,500
October to December	30,000
January 20X3 (30,000 × 1/3)	10,000
Rent for the year	100,000

Accrual 30,000 × 1/3 = 10,000

6   Diesel fuel charge = $87,700

Diesel fuel payable account		Cost of fuel used	
	$		$
Balance b/fwd	(1,700)	Opening inventory	12,500
Payments	85,400	Purchases	85,000
Balance c/fwd	1,300	Closing inventory	(9,800)
Purchases	85,000	Transfer to SPL	87,700

7   Telephone charge = $2,185

TELEPHONE ACCOUNT

	$		$
Prepayment b/f (2/3 × $90)	60	Accrual b/f	80
Bills paid	2,145	SPL account	2,185
Accrual c/f	120	Prepayment c/f (2/3 × $90)	60
	2,325		2,325

8   Rates charge for the year = $1,830

RATES ACCOUNT

	$		$
1.5.X1 Balance b/f		30.4.X2 Statement of profit or loss	1,830
(1,800 × 11/12)	1,650		
1.4.X2 Rates paid	2,160	30.4.X2 Balance c/f (2,160 × 11/12)	1,980
	3,810		3,810

9   Rent charge in the year = $1,300

RENT ACCOUNT

		$		$
1.5.X1	Rent paid	300	1.5.X1 Balance b/f	300
1.8.X1	Rent paid	300		
1.11. X1	Rent paid	300		
1.2.X2	Rent paid	300		
30.4/X2 Balance c/f (1,600/4)		400	30.4.X2 Statement of profit or loss	1,300
		1,600		1,600

An alternative calculation is:

	$
Rent charge 1.5.X1 to 31.1.X2	
(1,200 × 9/12)	900
Rent charge 1.2.X2 to 30.4.X2	
(1,600 × 3/12)	400
Total rent charge	1,300

10   D

	$
Accrual for Quarter 2 reversed	(1,600)
Gas bill paid	2,700
Accrual Quarter 3	2,400
Charge to statement of profit or loss Quarter 3	3,500

11 $1,850

1.7.20X1 – 31.3.20X2 1800 × 9/12 =	1,350
1.4.20X2 – 30.6.20X2 2000 × 3/12 =	500
	1,850

12 $22,000

Reconstruction of the trading account:

	$	$
Sales		40,000
Returns inwards		(2,000)
		38,000
Opening inventory	3,000	
Purchases	20,000	
Returns outwards	(4,000)	
Closing inventory	(3,000)	
		(16,000)
Gross profit		22,000

13   Rent payable = $6,000.

RENT PAYABLE ACCOUNT

		$			$
1.10.X5	Bal b/fwd	1,000	30.9.X6	Charge to SPL a/c	6,000
30.11.X5	Bank	1,500	30.9.X6	Rent prepaid c/fwd	
29.2.X6	Bank	1,500		(1500 × 2/3)	1,000
31.5.X6	Bank	1,500			
31.8.X6	Bank	1,500			
		7,000			7,000
1.10.X6	Rent prepaid b/fwd	1,000			

Alternatively, as you are told that the rent is $6,000 per annum and there has been no increase or decrease, this must be the annual charge.

14   Electricity charge = $5,000.

ELECTRICITY ACCOUNT

		$			$
5.11.X5	Bank	1,000	1.10.X5	Bal b/fwd	800
10.2.X6	Bank	1,300	30.9.X6	Charge to SPL a/c	5,000
8.5.X6	Bank	1,500			
7.8.X6	Bank	1,100			
30.9.X6	Accrual c/fwd	900			
		5,800			5,800
			1.10.X6	Balance b/fwd	900

15   Interest receivable = $850.

INTEREST RECEIVABLE ACCOUNT

		$			$
1.10.X5	Bal b/fwd	300	2.10.X5	Bank	250
30.9.X6	Transfer to SPL a/c	850	3.4.X6	Bank	600
			30.9.X6	Accrual c/fwd	300
		1,150			1,150
1.10.X6	Balance b/fwd	300			

11 Accounting for sales tax

1   B

SALES TAX CONTROL ACCOUNT

	$		$
		b/d	4,540
Purchases ($64,000 × 15%)	9,600	Sales ($109,250 × 15%/115%)	14,250
∴ Cash	11,910	c/d	2,720
	21,510		21,510

2   D   Alana is not registered for sales tax purposes and therefore cannot reclaim the input sales tax of $75.

3   C   Debit   Sales ledger control account $235
              Credit Sales $200
              Credit Sales tax control account $35

Working

Debit Sales ledger control account $235 (being net $200 plus sales tax $35; this can also be derived as the balancing figure)

Credit Sales $200 (being the net amount)

Credit Sales tax control account $35 (being the net $200 x 17.5%)

4   D

	$
Assets	
Opening cash	1,000
Cash received $(1,000 + 200 sales tax)	1,200
Closing cash	2,200
Inventory $(800 – 400)	400
	2,600
Liabilities	
Opening liabilities	–
Sales tax payable $(200 – 160)	40
Purchase inventory $(800 + 160 sales tax)	960
Closing liabilities	1,000
Capital	
Opening capital	1,000
Profit on sale of inventory $(1,000 – 400)	600
Closing capital	1,600

5   A   Receivables and payables include sales tax where applicable.

6   C   Tabby Co cannot reclaim input sales tax because they are exempt from charging sales tax on their sales.

7   C

	$
Output sales tax ($90,000 × 10%)	9,000
Input sales tax ($72,000 × 10%)	(7,200)
	1,800 payable

8   C

	$
Output tax (200,000 × 15%)	(30,000)
Input tax (161,000 × 15/115)	21,000
Payable	(9,000)

9   D $4,700 is payable. $700 goes to the sales tax control account in the statement of financial position.

10   D   A, B and C could all be reasons why the output tax does not equal 20% of sales. D is incorrect as it makes no difference whether the customer is registered for sales tax or not.

11   B   The sales tax element of the invoices will go to the sales tax account in the statement of financial position.

12   B

	$
Output sales tax $27,612.50 × $\frac{17.5}{117.5}$	4,112.50
Input sales tax $18,000 × $\frac{17.5}{100}$	3,150.00
∴ Balance on sales tax control account (credit)	962.50

13

Book of original entry	Debit entries		Credit entries	
	Account	$	Account	$
Purchase day book	Purchases	18,000		
	Sales tax	3,150	J Burgess	21,150

14

Book of original entry	Debit entries		Credit entries	
	Account	$	Account	$
Sales returns day book	Sales returns	400		
	Sales tax	70	J Lockley	470

15

Book of original entry	Debit entries		Credit entries	
	Account	$	Account	$
Purchases returns day book			Sales tax	84
	AS Supplies	564	Purchases	480

12 Accounting for payroll

1   A

	$
Net wages	15,000
Income tax	3,000
Employees NIC	1,650
Pension contribution	1,050
	20,700

2   C

Gross wage	440.00
PAYE income tax	(77.76)
Employees' NIC	(43.18)
Pension contribution (440.00 × 5%)	(22.00)
Net pay	297.06

3   D

4    $33,000

12 × $2,500 = $30,000 plus employer social security contributions of 10% = $3,000 therefore a total annual cost of $33,000. The employee income tax and employee social security contributions are deducted from gross wages by PY when paying this employee and are not an additional cost to the business.

5   B

	$
Net wages	240,000
Employee's tax	24,000
Employee's NI	12,000
Pension scheme contributions	6,000
Charitable donations	3,000
Gross wages	285,000
Employer's NI	14,000
	299,000

6

	$
36 × $3.50	126.00
Employer's NI	12.60
Gross wages cost (SPL account)	138.60
36 × $3.50	126.00
Tax (($126 – 75) × 20%)	(10.20)
Employees' NI	(8.82)
Paid to employee	106.98

7   D   Remember, employer's NI is an additional cost.

8   C $12,450 + $2,480 + $1,350 = $16,280

9   D   Gross wages = Income Tax + net wages + Employees NIC, plus the additional cost of Employers NIC taken to the SPL

= $17,000 + $50,000 + $6,000 + $7,500

10   D   The charge for the salary in the statement of profit or loss is the gross salary plus the employer's national insurance contribution. This is $1,500 plus $150 respectively, a total of $1,650.

11   A   Gross salary is charged to statement of profit or loss, debit wages and salaries expense, credit wages control account.

12   A   Employer's benefit contributions and employer's pension contributions form part of the overall cost of staff to the business. The total debited to staff costs is therefore $25,500 + $1,800 + $1,200 = $28,500.

13   Net pay is $7,043

	$
Gross pay	10,329
Employee's national insurance	626
Employee's pension deductions	546
Income tax	2,114
Net pay	7,043

14		Total payroll cost is $12,104		
				$
		Gross pay		10,329
		Employer's national insurance		1,054
		Employer's contribution to pension		721
				12,104

15	C	DEBIT	Wages control account	Employee national insurance deduction
		CREDIT	NIC control account	Employee national insurance deduction
		DEBIT	Employer's NIC (SPL)	Employer's national insurance
		CREDIT	NIC control account	Employer's national insurance

13 Bank reconciliations

1 B

	$
Balance per cash account	10,500 o/d
Add bank charges	175
Add transposition error	18
Adjusted cash account	10,693
Less uncleared cheques	(1,050)
	9,643 o/d

2 B

CASH BOOK

	$		$
Bal b/f	5,000	Payables (98% × 12,000)	11,760
Receivables	26,000	Bank charges	125
Cash sales	2,500	Bal c/f	21,615
	33,500		33,500

3 B $(565)o/d – $92 dishonoured cheque = $(657) o/d

The unpresented cheque has already been recorded in the cash book and therefore the bank balance per the statement of financial position does not require an adjustment for this.

4 B

	$
Original cash book figure	2,490
Adjustment re charges	(50)
Adjustment re dishonoured cheque	(140)
	2,300

5 A Dishonoured cheques and bank charges must be entered in the cash book.

6 B The only adjustment that should be made to the cash account is to record the bank charges. The cheques and lodgements will already have been recorded in the cash account.

7   D

	Cash $	Bank $
Balance	500	(1,000)
Receipts	12,600	
Contra	(5,500)	5,500
Paid	(3,200)	(8,200)
Drawings	(3,800)	(2,500)
Balance	600	(6,200)

(balancing figure) = total of $6,300

8   Cash book balance = $2,098 overdrawn

CASH BOOK

		$			$
31.5.X3	Balance b/d	873	31.5.X3	Bank charges	630
	Error $(936 – 693)	243		Direct debits	2,584
31.5.X3	Balance c/d	2,098			
		3,214			3,214
			1.6.X3	Balance b/d	2,098

9   Balance per bank statement = $974 (in credit)

BANK RECONCILIATION

	$
Balance per cash book	(901)
Outstanding lodgements	(593)
Unpresented cheques	2,468
Balance per bank statement	974

10   B

	$	$
Bank statement balance b/d	13,400	
Dishonoured cheque	300	
Bank charges not in cash book	50	
Unpresented cheques		2,400
Uncleared deposits	1,000	
Adjustment re error (2 × 195)		390
Cash book balance c/d		11,960
	14,750	14,750
Cash book balance b/d	11,960	

11   D   All the other options would have the bank account $250 less than the cash book.

12   D

	$
Balance per cash account	10,500 o/d
Less bank charges	175
Less transposition error	18
	10,693 o/d

13   C

14   Corrected cash book balance = $1,681 debit.

CASH BOOK

20X8		$	20X8		$
Dec 31	Balance b/d	1,793	Dec 31	Bank charges	18
Dec 31	Dividend	26	Dec 31	Standing order	32
			Dec 31	Direct debit	88
				Balance c/d	1,681
		1,819			1,819

15   **Add unrecorded lodgements** of $232

Deduct **unpresented cheques** of $108

BANK RECONCILIATION AS AT 31 DECEMBER 20X8

	$	$
Balance per bank statement		1,557
Add unrecorded lodgements:		
V Owen	98	
K Walters	134	
		232
Less unpresented cheques:		
B Oliver (869)	71	
L Philips (872)	37	
		(108)
Balance per cash book (corrected)		1,681

14 Control accounts

1   B   All of the other options would lead to a higher balance in the supplier's records.

2   C   The same error can still appear in the control account and the personal ledger.

3   D   A credit balance treated as a debit must be subtracted twice (ie $300). An omitted debit balance must be added once. Thus, the required adjustment to the list of balances is subtract $180; no adjustment is required to the sales ledger control account.

4   A   Remember, daybook totals are posted to the control account. Individual invoices are posted to the individual accounts, so an error in a total does not affect the list of balances.

5   B   Goods returned reduce what customers owe.

6

	DR	CR
	$	$
Discount allowed	32	
Receivables control account (PQ)		32

Sale price $800 – (20% × 800) = $640

Cash discount $640 × 5% = $32

7    $901

Cash discounts allowed should be credited. So a debit of $901 would result in an error of $1,802 between the ledger and the control account.

8   X is a receivable of Y or X owes Y.

9   Balance at 1 June 20X2 = $13,000

RECEIVABLES LEDGER CONTROL ACCOUNT

	$		$
Opening balance (bal fig)	13,000	Sales returns	6,200
Sales	164,500	Bank	155,300
		Discounts allowed	5,100
		Irrecoverable debts written off	2,600
		Closing balance	8,300
	177,500		177,500

10   C   Debits total $32,750 + $125,000 + $1,300 = $159,050.

Credits total $1,275 + $122,550 + $550 = $124,325.

Net balance = $34,725 debit.

11   A   If the day book was overcast, the total of the purchase invoices posted to the control account will be overstated.

The other options would increase the difference by reducing the total of purchase ledger balances.

12   C   Remember, daybook totals are posted to the control account. Individual invoices are posted to the individual accounts, so an error in a total does not affect the list of balances.

13   B

JOURNAL ENTRIES

		$ DR	$ CR
Error 1	Payables ledger control	420	
	Receivables ledger control		420
Error 4	Irrecoverable debts	240	
	Receivables ledger control		240
Error 5	Sales	900	
	Receivables ledger control		900

14   C

BALANCES EXTRACTED FROM THE RECEIVABLES LEDGER

		+ $	− $	$
Total before corrections for errors				15,800
Error 2	Mahmood	90		
Error 3	Yasmin	780		
Error 6	Charles		300	
Error 7	Edward	125		
		995	300	695
				16,495

15   C

RECEIVABLES LEDGER CONTROL ACCOUNT

	$			$
∴ Balance b/f	17,560	Error 1	Ahmed	420
		Error 4	Thomas	240
		Error 5	Sales daybook total	900
				1,560
			Balance c/f	16,000
	17,560			17,560

15 Correction of errors

1   A

SUSPENSE ACCOUNT

	$		$
Balance b/d	210	Gas bill (420 – 240)	180
Interest	70	Discount (2 × 50)	100
	280		280

2   C   A is an error of omission, B is an error of principle, D is a transposition error.

3   B   The posting is correct, but the wrong amount has been used.

4   C   This is a posting made to the wrong class of account.

5   A   Closing inventory is entered twice in an extended trial balance (once for the statement of profit or loss and once for the statement of financial position). It is not included in a trial balance, which, of course, balanced without it!

6   B   Opening inventory is a debit balance.

7   B   The journal for this transaction is debit drawings and credit purchases. Thus, profit rises and net assets stay the same.

8   A   The journal for this correction is debit non-current assets, credit purchases. Thus, profit and net assets are increased.

9   D   Reclassifying a liability as long term rather than current, will increase net current assets, but has no effect on current assets or net assets.

10   D   This inventory should be included at the lower of cost and net realisable value, causing profits to rise by $5,000.

11   C   Cost of sales is $1,300 understated and expenses $1,000 understated.

12   B   A two debits error has occurred with $1,250 debited to both the advertising account and the bank account without a corresponding credit entry.

To correct the imbalance of $2,500, the bank account must be credited with $1,250 to reverse the original incorrect debit of $1,250 and then credited with a further $1,250 to correctly include this amount on the credit side of the account.

The correcting journal would be:
DR Suspense $2,500
CR Bank $2,500

     A   Incorrect, this is a reversal of entries error with a corresponding debit and credit entry. It would be corrected as:
DR Rent $5,000
CR Bank $5,000

     C   Incorrect, an error of omission cannot create a difference in the trial balance.

     D   Incorrect, this is also a reversal of entries error.

13

		$	$
DR	Trade receivables	300	
CR	Trade payables		300

14

		$	$
DR	Heat and light	300	
CR	Suspense account		300

15

		$	$
DR	G Gordon	800	
CR	G Goldman		800

16 Incomplete records

1   C

	$	
Sales	21,950	(100%)
Less cost of sales	17,560	(80%)
Gross profit	4,390	(20%)

Receivables			
B/d	3,050	Cash	21,000
Sales	21,950	C/d	4,000
	25,000		25,000

2	D			
			$	
		Sales	36,400	(130%)
		Less cost of sales	28,000	(100%)
		Gross profit	8,400	
		Less expenses	(14,000)	
		Net loss	5,600	

3   A   Gross profit is $25,500 − $21,250 = $4,250, which is 16.67% of $25,500.

4   B

	$
Opening capital (balancing figure)	5,400
Capital introduced	9,800
Profits	8,000
	23,200
Drawings	(4,200)
	19,000

5   C

CASH ACCOUNT

	$		$
Balance b/d	300	Bankings (50,000 − 5,000)	45,000
		Wages	12,000
		Drawings	24,000
Takings (bal fig)	81,100	Balance c/d	400
	81,400		81,400

6   A   The other options would make the credit side total $50 more than the debit side.

7   Closing inventory = $500

	$
Sales (100%)	15,000
Gross profit (30%)	4,500
Cost of goods sold (70%)	10,500
Opening inventory	1,000
Purchases (from previous question)	10,000
	11,000
Cost of goods sold	10,500
Closing inventory (balancing figure)	500

8   C $1,370

Cash account

	$		$
Balance b/d	900	Cash expenses	2,400
Cash sales	3,550	Petty cash β	1,370
	–	Balance c/d	680
	4,450		4,450

9   B

	$
Net assets 31/12/X1:	
2,000 + 500 + 300 − 50 + 200	2,950
Net assets 31/12/X2:	
2,500 + 100 + 50 − 600 − 100 + 250	2,200
Decrease in net assets	750

From the accounting equation:

$$\text{Change in net assets} = \text{Capital} + \text{profit} - \text{drawings}$$

$$-750 = \text{Profit} - \text{drawings (\$1,000)}$$

$$-750 + 1,000 = \text{Profit}$$

$$250 = \text{Profit}$$

10   B   Drawings reduce capital, so they must be deducted.

11   A

	$	$
Sales		25,500 (100%)
Opening inventory	3,675	
Purchases	22,000	
Less closing inventory	(4,000)	
Cost of sales		21,675 (85%)
Gross profit		3,825 (15%)

12   B

	$	$
Sales		25,500 (120%)
Opening inventory	5,250	
Purchases	26,000	
Less closing inventory	(10,000)	
Cost of sales		21,250 (100%)
Gross profit		4,250 (20%)

13   A   The business equation is Net assets = Capital + Profit − Drawings.

14   C

TOTAL RECEIVABLES ACCOUNT

	$		$
Opening balance	130,000	Cash received	686,400
Sales (balancing figure)	744,960	Discounts allowed	1,400
		Irrecoverable debts	4,160
		Contra	2,000
		Closing balance	181,000
	874,960		874,960

TOTAL PAYABLES ACCOUNT

	$		$
Cash paid	302,800	Opening balance	60,000
Discounts received	2,960	Purchases (balancing figure)	331,760
Contra	2,000		
Closing balance	84,000		
	391,760		391,760

17 Limited company financial statements

1   B

Inventories are a current asset. Prepaid expenses are payments made in advance and so they are an asset. Tax owed by the tax authorities to a company is also an asset as it is money that will be received in the next financial period.

A bank overdraft and trade payables are current liabilities.

2   D   2, 4 and 5

A revaluation gain is not reported in profit for the year or the cash flow statement as the gain is not yet realised and the cash has not been received. The property may not be sold or the market value may fall in the future therefore it is not certain that the gain will ever be realised and should therefore be reported as other comprehensive income.

3   D   Loan stock is a non-current liability.

The share premium account, retained earnings and revaluation surplus account are shown under 'equity'.

4   B   The statement of changes in equity.

5   A   Correct $500,000 \times 15\% = \$75,000$

B   Incorrect, interest paid and accrued comprise the total expense for the year.

C   Incorrect, only half a year's interest is outstanding.

D   Incorrect, this represents 18 months interest.

6   D   The revaluation surplus is part of equity. A loan due for repayment within one year, taxation and accrued expenses are current liabilities.

7   D   This is a distribution of reserves.

8   A   Non-current liabilities do not form part of the equity capital of a limited company.

9   B

	$
Interim ordinary dividends (5c × 400,000)	20,000
Preference dividend ((50,000 × $2 × 5%)/2)	2,500
Paid to date	22,500
Final ordinary dividend (15c × 400,000)	60,000
Preference dividend (must be paid before final ordinary dividend)	2,500
	85,000

10   C   A reduction in the allowance for receivables reduces administration expenses and depreciation of machinery and the production director's salary would increase cost of sales.

18 Issues of shares

1   B

		$
Ordinary shares		
Opening balance		125,000
Rights issue	250,000 × 25c	62,500
Bonus issue	150,000 × 25c	37,500
		225,000
Share premium		
Opening balance		100,000
Rights issue	250,000 × 75c	187,500
Bonus issue	150,000 × 25c	(37,500)
		250,000

2   B   This is the transfer of the premium to the share premium account.

3   B   The total will be $260,000, of which $60,000 will be credited to share premium.

4   C

	$
Share capital @ 1.1.20X0	500,000
Issue on 1.4.20X0 (200,000 @ 50c)	100,000
Bonus issue (1.2m ÷ 4) @ 50c	150,000
Share capital as at 31.12.20X0	750,000
Share premium @ 1.1.20X0	300,000
1.4.20X0 200,000 shares @ (130c − 50c)	160,000
Bonus issue (as above)	(150,000)
	310,000

5   A   A rights issue will increase cash and therefore assets. Retained earnings remain the same and the share premium account will be increased.

6   D   2, 4 and 5

7   B   False

A bonus issue is the issue of extra shares to existing shareholders at no cost. A bonus issue does not raise any additional finance.

8   Amended retained earnings = $69,000

	$
Draft retained earnings	84,000
Adjustment for closing inventory	(10,000)
Transfer to general reserve	(5,000)
	69,000

9	Share capital (200,000 + 50,000)	250,000
10	Share premium (40,000 + 30,000)	70,000
	General reserve (20,000 + 5,000)	25,000

19 Manufacturing accounts

1   Factory cost of goods completed = $96,800.

	$
Purchases of raw materials	56,000
Increase in inventories of raw materials	(1,700)
Direct wages	21,000
Carriage inwards	2,500
Production overheads	14,000
Decrease in work-in-progress	5,000
Factory cost of sales	96,800

2   C   Prime cost includes all **direct** costs of production.

3   A

	$	$
Raw materials		
Opening inventory	10,000	
Purchases	50,000	
Closing inventory	(11,000)	
Cost of raw materials		49,000
Direct wages		40,000
Prime cost		89,000
Production overheads		60,000
		149,000
Increase in work in progress 4,000 – 2,000		
Cost of goods manufactured		147,000

4   D   This is because some of the WIP has been consumed to complete those goods.

5   D   Only **direct** costs are included in prime cost.

6   B   Indirect cost

7   D

8   The gross profit for the year is $94,000

	$
Opening inventory of raw materials	18,000
Purchases	163,000
	181,000
Less closing inventory of raw materials	(21,000)
Raw materials used	160,000
Manufacturing expenses	115,000
Factory cost of goods produced	275,000

	$	$
Sales		365,000
Less: Cost of goods sold		
Opening finished goods inventory	34,000	
Factory cost of goods produced	275,000	
	309,000	
Less closing inventory of finished goods	(38,000)	
		(271,000)
Gross profit		94,000

9   A   Correct.

    B   Incorrect, no adjustment for work in progress has been made.

    C   This excludes production overheads.

    D   Prime cost has already been adjusted for changes in raw material inventory levels.

10   B

	$
Purchase of raw materials	112,000
Decrease in inventory of raw materials	8,000
Carriage inwards	3,000
Raw materials used	123,000
Direct wages	42,000
Prime cost	165,000
Production overheads	27,000
Increase in WIP	(10,000)
Factory cost of finished goods	182,000

11   $735,000

	$'000
Prime cost	360
Factory indirect overheads	450
Increase in inventory – work in progress	(75)
Factory cost of goods completed	735

12   C

Prime cost	56,000
Factory overheads	4,500
Opening WIP	6,200
Factory cost of	(57,000)
Therefore closing WIP is	9,700

13   Prime cost for the year ended 31 December 20X5 = $115,000

	$
Opening inventory	25,000
Purchases	80,000
	105,000
Less closing inventory	(24,000)
Raw materials used	81,000
Direct wages	34,000
Prime cost	115,000

14   Total depreciation charge for the year ended 31 December 20X5 = $9,000

	Non-current assets at cost $	Carrying value $	Accumulated depreciation $
At 31 December 20X4	60,000	39,000	21,000
At 31 December 20X5	90,000	60,000	30,000
Depreciation charge for the year			9,000

15   The factory cost of goods completed during the year ended 31 December 20X6 was $447,000

	$
Prime cost	720,000
Factory overheads	72,000
Add opening work in progress	5,000
Less closing work in progress	(350,000)
Factory cost of goods completed	447,000

20 Statements of cash flows

1   A   Cash flows from operating activities are adjusted to reflect interest actually paid in the period.

2   B

NON-CURRENT ASSETS AT COST

	$'000		$'000
Balance b/d	25	Disposal	10
Additions (bal fig)	15	Balance c/d	30
	40		40

	$'000
Disposal – carrying value	2
Profit on disposal	2
Proceeds	4

Net cash inflow = $15,000 – 4,000 = $11,000

3   D

	$'000	$'000
Loss on sale of machinery		
Carrying value (10 – 6)	4	
Disposal proceeds	(1)	
Loss on disposal		3
Depreciation charge for the year		8
Total to add back to operating profit		11

4 A The reduction in the overdraft is an increase in cash of $4,000.

The reduction in short term investments (of $10,000) would be included in movement in cash equivalents

5      $15,000 inflow

	Inflow	Outflow
Reduction in inventory	40,000	
Increase in receivables		20,000
Increase in trade payables	10,000	
Reduction in other payables		15,000
	50,000	35,000
Net inflow	15,000	

6 A Financing cash flow = issue of shares + share premium received + proceeds of rights issue – loan repaid.

The interest paid is included in operating activities.

	$'000
Issues of shares	500
Share premium received	150
Proceeds of rights issue	350
Total inflows	1,000
Loan repaid	(250)
Net inflow	750

7 A Cash flow = sale proceeds – purchases = 300,000 – 1,500,000 = 1,200,000 outflow.
Sale proceeds = carrying value + profit = 250,000 + 50,000 = 300,000

Depreciation is not a movement of cash.

8 B The purchase of non-current assets is an investing activity.

9 C The issues of shares provides finance to the company and so is a financing activity.

10 C

Increase in inventory	(6,000)
Decrease in receivables	2,000
Decrease in payables	(3,000)
Net adjustment	(7,000)

11 C Only the proceeds of a share issue and dividends received involve the movement of cash.

12 D Loss on sale of non-current assets should be added back to net profit before tax.

13	$48,900		
			31.12.X2
			$
	Property, plant and equipment at the start of the year		210,000
	Additions β		48,900
	Depreciation charge		(18,900)
	Property, plant and equipment at the end of the year		240,000

14	$18,000		
			31.12.X2
			$
	Opening tax liability		21,000
	Tax charge		22,000
	Cash paid β		(18,000)
	Closing tax liability		25,000

15	$16,000		
			31.12.X2
			$
	Opening cash		124,000
	Increase in cash β		16,000
	Closing cash		140,000

21 Interpreting company accounts

1   D

	%	$
Sales	150	180,000
Cost of sales	100	(120,000)
Gross profit	50	60,000

$$\therefore \text{ Inventory turnover} = \frac{120,000}{(12,000+18,000)/2} = 8 \text{ times}$$

2   A $\dfrac{\text{Cost of sales}}{\text{Average inventory}} = \dfrac{\$24,500}{(4,000+6,000) \div 2} = 4.9 \text{ times}$

3   A   Non-current loans raise gearing, shareholders funds reduce it.

4   C   Current ratio is 2,900 : 1,100 = 2.6: 1 ie high

Acid test ratio is 1,000 : 1,100 = 0.9 ie acceptable

5   C

	$
Sales	100,800
Cost of sales	(72,000)
∴ Gross profit	28,800

$$\text{Gross profit mark-up} = \frac{\$28,800}{\$72,000} \times 100 = 40\%$$

6   D   Purchases $= \$(32{,}500 - 6{,}000 + 3{,}800)$

$$= \$30{,}300$$

$$\therefore \text{Payables' payment period} = \frac{4{,}750}{30{,}300} \times 365 = 57 \text{ days}$$

7   A $\text{Gearing} = \dfrac{\text{long-term}}{\text{long-term + equity}} = \dfrac{75}{75 + 500} = 13\%$

8   C $\dfrac{\text{Current assets}}{\text{Current liabilitites}}$

9   B   Current assets are normally inventory, receivables, bank. Current liabilities are normally payables, overdraft.

10   A   Inventory holding 2 months + 0.5 months in WIP + 3 months in finished goods inventory + 3 months receivable payment less 2 months credit from suppliers.

11   C   Correct, inventory, receivables, prepayments, cash.

Cash is the most liquid asset, followed by prepayments, trade receivables and finally inventory. Inventory must be sold before being turned into cash and is therefore the least liquid of these options

12   B

	%	%
Revenue	100	2,400
Cost of sales	66.67	1,600
Gross profit	33.33	800
Expenses	28.33	680
Net profit	5.00	120

13   C   Non-current asset turnover is $\dfrac{\text{Turnover}}{\text{Non-current assets}} = \dfrac{\$12{,}000}{\$4{,}700} = 2.553 \text{ times}$

14   D $\text{Gross profit margin} = \dfrac{\text{Gross profit}}{\text{Turnover}} \times 100 = \dfrac{\$5{,}000}{\$12{,}000} \times 100$

$$= 42\%$$

15   C   Inventory days are $\dfrac{\text{Inventory}}{\text{Cost of sales}} \times 365 = \dfrac{1{,}200}{7{,}000} \times 365$

$$= 63 \text{ days}$$

Receivable days are $\dfrac{\text{Receivables}}{\text{Turnover}} \times 365 = \dfrac{1{,}700}{12{,}000} \times 365$

$$= 52 \text{ days}$$

22 The Framework

1   A   Statement (1) only is correct.

Materiality concerns whether an item in the financial statements can influence users' decisions. Information should be a faithful representation of the economic phenomena it purports to represent. This includes being neutral, ie without bias in the selection or presentation of the financial information. Therefore information must not be manipulated in any way in order to influence the decisions of the users.

2   C   The accruals concept.

3   C   The materiality concept.

4   D

5   D   A revaluation surplus will be presented as part of equity, not current liabilities.

6   C   Information has the quality of faithful representation when it is complete, neutral and free from material error.

7   A   Depreciation allocates the cost of an asset to the periods expected to benefit from its use.

8   B   Accruals. The stationery must be charged to the period in which it was consumed.

9   A   Comparability can usually be achieved through consistency and disclosure.

10   D   Social and relationship capital is defined by the IIRC as 'the institutions and the relationships within and between communities, groups of stakeholders and other networks, and the ability to share information to enhance individual and collective well-being'.

Natural capital is 'renewable and non-renewable environmental resources and processes'.

Financial capital is 'the pool of funds that is available to an organisation for use in production of goods or services and obtained through financing, such as debt, equity or grants, or generated through operations or investments.'

Human capital is 'people's competencies, capabilities and experience, and their motivations to innovate'.

11   A   The separate entity concept applies here, so that these expenses are treated as drawings and not part of the business expenses.

12   1   Going concern
     2   Accruals

13   NO.

This suggestion is flawed. Obsolete inventory should be provided for under the concept of consistency.

14   NO

This suggestion is flawed. If no depreciation is allowed for, this assumes that there is no reduction in useful life over the past year (which is very unlikely). Therefore not to allow for depreciation is inconsistent.

15   NO

This suggestion is flawed. Accounting standards require research costs to be written off in the year they are incurred.

23 The regulatory system

1   D   The IFRS Foundation oversees the standard setting and regulatory process and the International Accounting Standards Board formulate international financial reporting standards.

2   C   To provide instructions as to how items should be shown in a set of financial statements

3   A

4   C   This is one of the IASB's key objectives.

5   B   This is one of the IASB's key objectives.

6   C   The role of the IASB is to develop and publish International Financial Reporting Standards.

7   B   The role of the IASB is to develop and publish international financial reporting standards.

8   A   The IFRS Advisory Council.

9   C   The IFRS Interpretations Committee assists the IASB in identifying financial reporting issues not specifically addressed in IFRSs.

10   D   The members of the IFRS Advisory Council, the International Accounting Standards Board and the IFRS Interpretations Committee are all appointed by the IFRS Foundation.

11   D   One of the objectives of the IFRS Foundation is to bring about convergence of national accounting standards and IFRSs.

12   The IFRS **Interpretations Committee** issues **IFRS interpretations** which aid users' interpretation of IFRSs.

13   B   Taxation authorities do not provide regulation on the financial statements of companies.

        The Stock Exchange provides requirements for quoted companies only.

14   C   The IFRS Foundation does not focus primarily on the needs of global, multi-national organisations. One of the objectives of the foundation is to take account of the financial reporting needs of emerging economies and small and medium-sized entities (SMEs).

15   A   One of the ways IFRSs are used is as an international benchmark for those countries which develop their own requirements.

Review Form – Paper BA3 Fundamentals of Financial Accounting

Please help us to ensure that the CIMA learning materials we produce remain as accurate and user-friendly as possible. We cannot promise to answer every submission we receive, but we do promise that it will be read and taken into account when we update this Exam Practice Kit

Name: _____   Address: _____

_____

_____

How have you used this Exam Practice Kit?
(Tick one box only)

☐ Home study (book only)

☐ On a course: college _____

☐ Other _____

Why did you decide to purchase this Exam Practice Kit? *(Tick one box only)*

☐ Have used BPP learning materials in the past

☐ Recommendation by friend/colleague

☐ Recommendation by a lecturer at college

☐ Saw information on BPP website

☐ Saw advertising

☐ Other _____

Which BPP products have you used?

Text   ☐

Kit   ☑

Passcard ☐

Do you intend to continue using BPP products?   *Yes*   *No*

The BPP author of this edition can be e-mailed at: lmfeedback@bpp.com

Review Form (continued)

TELL US WHAT YOU THINK

Please note any further comments and suggestions/errors below